First published in 2015 by Voyageur Press, an imprint of Quarto Publishing Group USA Inc., 400 First Avenue North, Suite 400, Minneapolis, MN 55401 USA

© 2015 Quarto Publishing Group USA Inc.
Text © 2015 Brian Solomon

All rights reserved. With the exception of quoting brief passages for the purposes of review, no part of this publication may be reproduced without prior written permission from the Publisher.

The information in this book is true and complete to the best of our knowledge. All recommendations are made without any guarantee on the part of the author or Publisher, who also disclaims any liability incurred in connection with the use of this data or specific details.

Voyageur Press titles are also available at discounts in bulk quantity for industrial or sales-promotional use. For details write to Special Sales Manager at Quarto Publishing Group USA Inc., 400 First Avenue North, Suite 400, Minneapolis, MN 55401 USA.

To find out more about our books, visit us online at www.voyageurpress.com.

ISBN: 978-0-7603-4692-1

Acquisitions Editor: Dennis Pernu and Steve Casper
Design Manager: James Kegley
Layout: Danielle Smith-Boldt

Cover photo: Union Switch & Signal color light signals make for a stunning lunar silhouette on CSX's former Chesapeake & Ohio line at Vauces, Ohio. *John Leopard*

Printed in China
10 9 8 7 6 5 4 3 2 1

CLASSIC RAILROAD SIGNALS

Semaphores, Searchlights, and Towers

Brian Solomon

Voyageur Press

DEDICATION

In Memory of "Uncle" Harry Vallas

CONTENTS

DEDICATION 4

INTRODUCTION TO AMERICAN SIGNALING 6

1 AMERICAN SIGNALING BASICS 11

2 TOWERS AND INTERLOCKING SIGNALS 35

3 TWO-POSITION SEMAPHORES 53

4 UPPER-QUADRANT SEMAPHORES 67

5 COLOR LIGHTS 95

6 POSITION LIGHT SIGNALS 119

7 GRADE CROSSING PROTECTION AND UNUSUAL RAILROAD SIGNALS 135

ACKNOWLEDGMENTS 150

BIBLIOGRAPHY 152

GLOSSARY 155

INDEX 157

INTRODUCTION TO AMERICAN SIGNALING

Signals have been a fundamental part of railroad operating rules since the nineteenth century. For decades, semaphores, color lights, searchlights, and position lights have provided railroads with vital operating instructions. North American railway signaling is a complex and fascinating topic owing to differences in philosophy, a variety of hardware, and varying degrees of signal protection required by different railway companies. In 1912, *The Signal Engineer*—a trade magazine published for the benefit of signaling professionals—wrote that "The language of signaling is expressive and picturesque to a high degree."

Railway signaling is necessary because of fundamental restrictions in the movement of trains. Track space is limited, and unlike road vehicles, trains moving at speed cannot stop within the limits of sight and thus require advanced warning to stop safely. The essence of most signaling is to provide safe separation between trains moving in the same direction, to provide absolute protection for opposing movements on single track, and to prevent trains from occupying conflicting routes at junctions, crossings, and other places where routes interface or require absolute protection.

The messages supplied by signals are simple operating instructions, yet because signaling systems evolved gradually over the years, the means and methods for delivering messages and the specific information conveyed have varied both among different lines and over time.

Efforts at reconciling incongruities and differences in practice have produced standard means of interpreting signals and have limited the varieties of hardware, yet considerable variety in signal practices has remained. Even where standards prevail there have been numerable exceptions. An established practice on one road might be an exceptional situation on another. Comparison of rules between lines over the decades reveals dozens of different approaches to operational situations, sometimes offering confusing, if not conflicting, signaling solutions.

This book covers American line-side signal hardware as employed by classic railroads in the twentieth century. I've presented signaling history and development, along with some of the key personalities involved. In addition to discussing general principles, I've highlighted specific applications and exceptions while discussing the information signals have conveyed and how it has been interpreted by various railroad rulebooks over time. Virtually every major railroad had some distinguishing signal practice or hardware.

My primary focus is on the signals and their history, the aspects and indications, and how these relate to operations. I've not dwelt any more than necessary on vital technology such as track circuits, relays, solid-state advancements, or other control mechanisms. Nor have I delved into the various forms of advance signaling such as automatic train stop, cab signals, or modern positive train control systems. For those interested in a more general discussion, my book, *Railroad Signaling* (published by MBI in 2003), covers signaling technology and applications from the earliest days through recent contemporary development and application.

Most of the styles of signal hardware used in North America during the classic period (loosely defined as from World War I to the advent of large mergers in the 1960s and 1970s) had been refined by 1927. After that date, signaling innovation was largely focused on control mechanisms and refinements of railroad rules.

The necessity to provide all-weather, fail-safe, and reliable equipment that required minimal maintenance resulted in exceptionally rugged and unusually durable line-side signal hardware. Signaling was expensive, and railroads' reluctance to invest any more than necessary in non-revenue producing systems often resulted in exceptional longevity for established signaling systems. Line-side signals have had a tendency to last much longer than rolling stock. In modern times signals have outlasted most of the individual railroad companies that installed them. So, many of the images in this book are relatively contemporary, which demonstrates the long life of signaling hardware.

Through the early years of the twenty-first century, classic signal systems have survived as a legacy of the early- and mid-twentieth century. Incredibly, signals dating from the steam era have continued to function for decades after the last steam locomotives were retired from revenue service in the 1950s.

Up through the 1990s, many new installations used styles of hardware developed during the innovative period between 1900 and 1927. As of 2014, while signals are less varied, many surviving types of hardware still have roots in technology refined during the World War I era.

Signal hardware has been some of the most enduring equipment on railroads. This Federal Signal Company relay case at Earlville, Illinois, dates from sometime between the company's 1908 name change and when it was absorbed by General Railway Signal Company in 1923. BNSF Railway predecessor Chicago, Burlington & Quincy was a large user of Federal lower-quadrant semaphores and interlocking equipment. *John Leopard*

Despite this, twentieth-century signaling is rapidly fading from the scene. The necessity to implement modern signaling systems, especially federally mandated positive train control systems, is rapidly taking its toll on traditional hardware. Old control systems such as manual block have already all but vanished from operating practices, semaphores are nearly extinct, and change is rapidly catching up with 1920s-era color light hardware. The searchlight, position light, and color position light signals that had characterized signal

After nearly a century, old Monon semaphores had finally reached the end of their service. In recent years, as the date to fulfill positive train control mandate approached, Class 1 railroads have rapidly replaced "legacy hardware"—twentieth century signaling—with modern systems. On December 4, 2010, CSX 1560 approaches Crawfordsville, Indiana. *Chris Guss*

systems for decades are not only largely out of favor, but rapidly disappearing from the scene. Surviving signals that have enjoyed great longevity will soon be swept aside.

Throughout the twentieth century, the traditional manufacturers, General Railway Signal and Union Switch & Signal, had supplied the majority of signaling hardware. This is no longer true as a variety of new firms now supply signal systems and hardware. Modern signaling equipment must be compatible with the latest control systems, and in some situations even relatively modern hardware is also being replaced with the latest technology. Traditional bulb-lit signal heads are being replaced with signals using light-emitting diodes (LEDs), while consolidation of rulebooks is gradually minimizing the variety of aspects.

This book offers a look back at classic signaling while there's still an opportunity to experience the old signals at work. If a signaling enthusiast had a time machine, turning back the clock to the period between 1910 and 1925 would offer the opportunity to study the greatest variety of practices and hardware.

A General Railway Signal Company Model MF dwarf signal displays "stop" at Jordon Street Interlocking on Kansas City Southern's Shreveport Terminal Subdivision in Shreveport, Louisiana. Since the 1920s, Centralized Traffic Control signaling has become a dominant method for authorizing train movements on American mainlines. *Chris Guss*

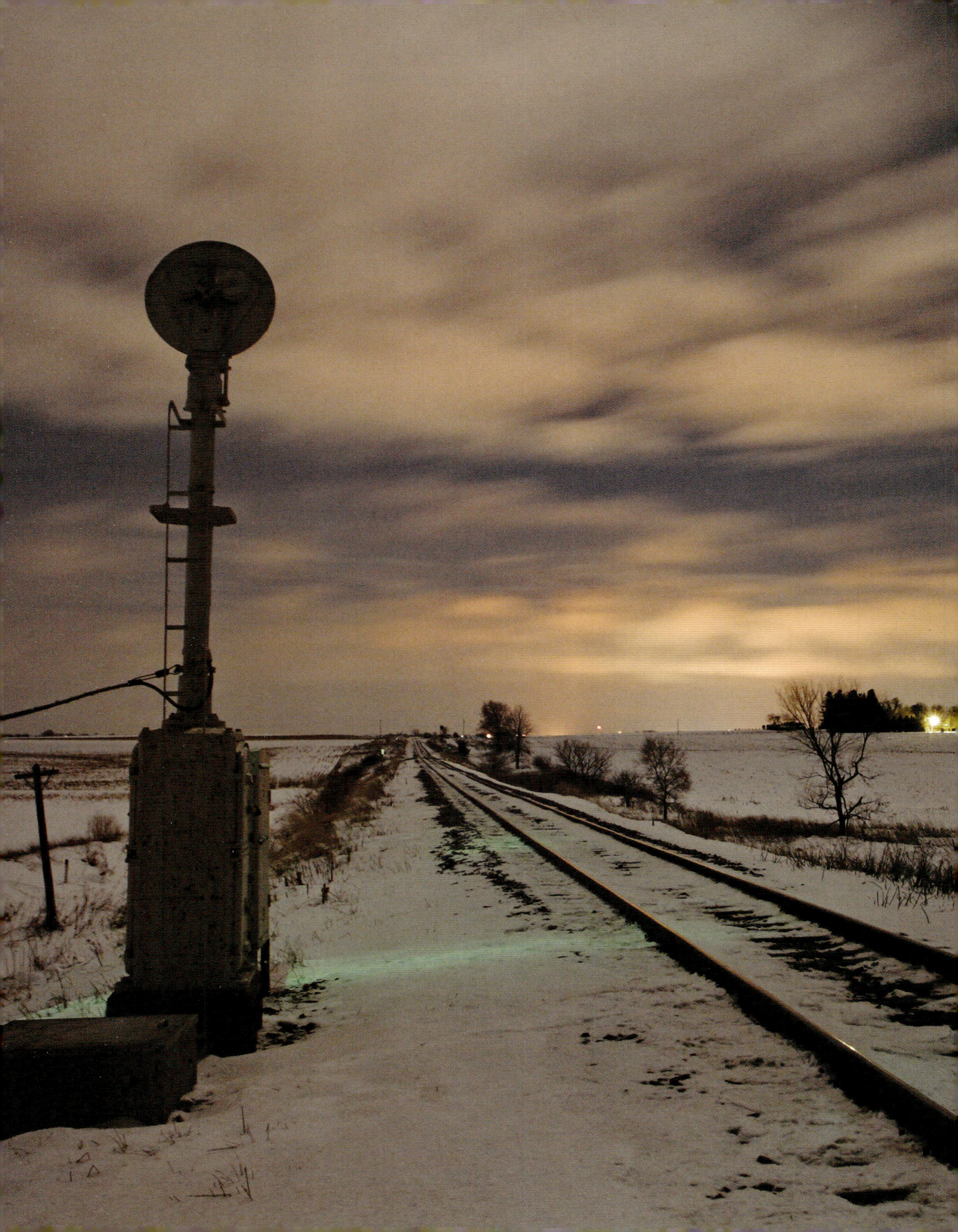

AMERICAN SIGNALING BASICS

1

Essentials for Safety

Green for "Proceed" and red for "Stop"—what could be simpler than that? But green hasn't always indicated "Proceed," and there's a lot more than these two simple instructions in the language of railroad signaling.

Signaling is necessary to govern track usage. Complicating matters in regards to this system are railroad braking distances that greatly exceed the limits of sight. Quite simply, train crews need absolute authority to run on main lines and require advance warning to allow them to safely control train speed. This is a balancing act: if trains move too quickly they won't be able to stop safely, but if they travel too conservatively the whole system becomes inefficient and ineffective. Slow-moving trains reduce capacity. Particularly troublesome are junctions, where track space is at a premium and trains may need to travel over various routes at differing speeds.

Fixed signal rules evolved from hand signaling with colored flags, which itself evolved from maritime semaphore practices. American railway rules, particularly those relating to train movements, have their origins in British practice. American railroad signaling evolved in various ways. Signaling started out simple. But as companies grew and operations became more complex, operational rules evolved to meet specific situations. When each railroad company's operations were largely independent from one another, disparity in rules had little affect

All signals show clear on the former Rock Island Lines on December 10, 2005. These Union Switch & Signal Style TP-5 color lights from the Rock Island era protect Union Pacific's Mason City Subdivision north of Iowa Falls, Iowa. The Style TP-5 was among several triangular pattern color lights used on North American railways. *Chris Guss*

SIGNAL INDICATIONS.

501cc.

Fig. 61   Fig. 62   Fig. 63   Fig. 64   Fig. 65

Fig. 66   Fig. 67   Fig. 68   Fig. 69

Indication—Proceed.
Name—Clear-Signal.

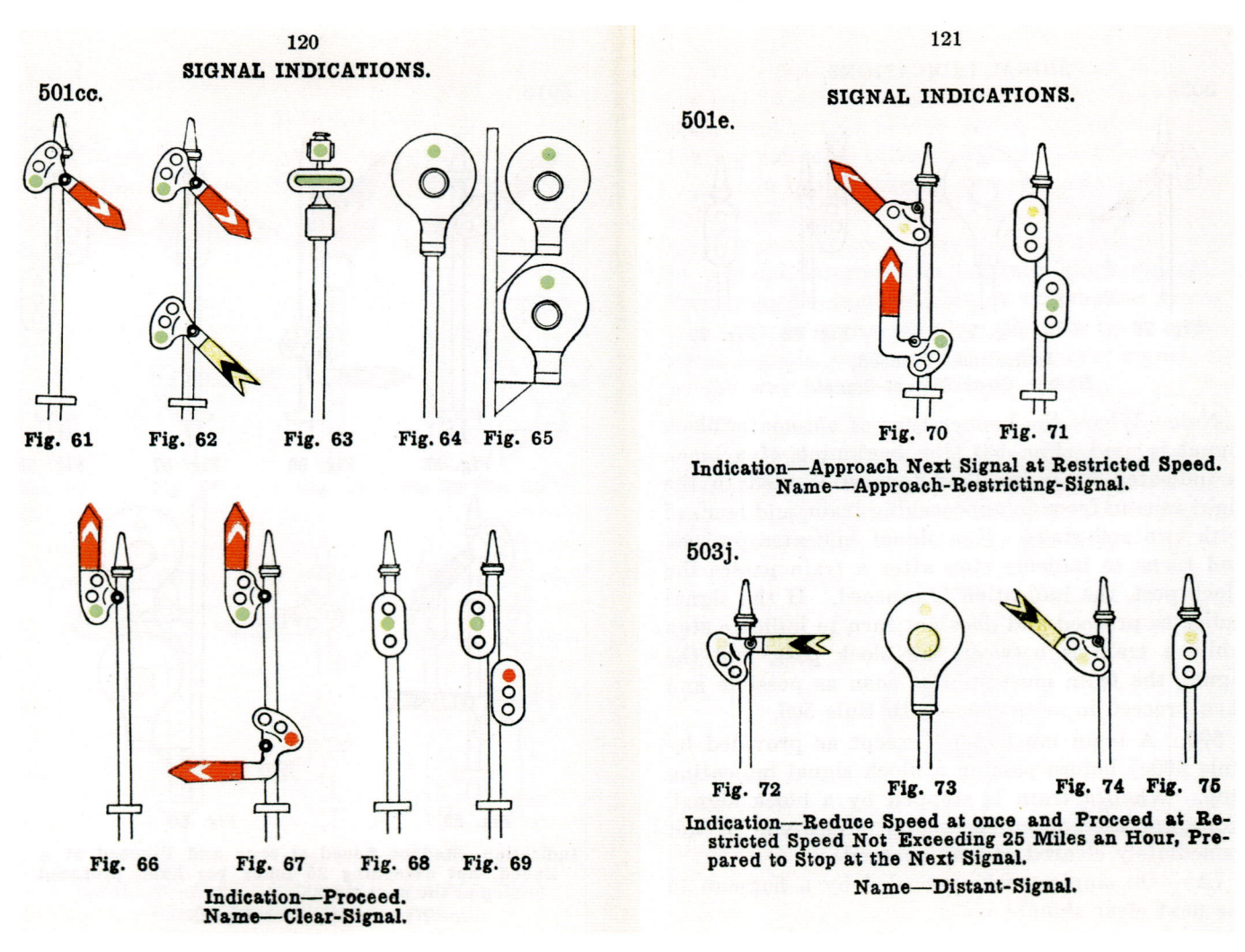

SIGNAL INDICATIONS.

501e.

Fig. 70   Fig. 71

Indication—Approach Next Signal at Restricted Speed.
Name—Approach-Restricting-Signal.

503j.

Fig. 72   Fig. 73   Fig. 74   Fig. 75

Indication—Reduce Speed at once and Proceed at Restricted Speed Not Exceeding 25 Miles an Hour, Prepared to Stop at the Next Signal.
Name—Distant-Signal.

New Haven Railroad's January 1, 1925, rulebook reflects the diversity of hardware in service on the company's lines. New Haven was unusual because it had Hall disc signals, upper- and lower-quadrant semaphores, and color lights in block service at the same time. *Collection of the Irish Railway Record Society*

on safety practices, but as railroads began interfacing, their incongruous and sometimes contradictory operating rules posed serious safety concerns.

Train speeds and traffic volumes increased rapidly during the late nineteenth and early twentieth centuries, placing ever-greater demands on track space and increasing both the likelihood, and severity, of accidents. As accidents grew more common and their results more gruesome, the public and government became increasingly intolerant of mishaps. Reluctantly, railroads recognized the need to invest in systems of accident avoidance. Interlocking and block signaling schemes simultaneously offered the most cost effective means of preventing accidents while safely increasing line capacity. (A signaling scheme is a system of signal hardware that displays predetermined sequences of aspects to convey specific operating information.)

Advances in electrical technology and communications provided many new tools for signal manufacturers. The invention and development of the track circuit and electrically operated hardware allowed for sophisticated block systems and more effective interlocking control. (A track circuit is an electric control mechanism used to detect a train, track condition, or track defect in order to actuate a signal system). To understand how signal systems instruct train crews, it helps to appreciate the differing philosophies and approaches to signaling practice during its formative years.

12   Chapter 1

Basic Signaling

The appearance of a signal is called its aspect. Each aspect has a name, such as "Clear," and an *indication*, such as "Proceed," which is the information conveyed by the aspect and clearly defined in a railroad's rulebook.

Over the years there has been considerable disparity in the aspects displayed and the specifics of their indications. Since there are many different aspects used to give any specific indication, this chapter will focus first on indications; later chapters will detail various aspects.

This old Hall Signal Company lower-quadrant semaphore was photographed in December 1992, near Center Rutland, Vermont, on the former Delaware & Hudson. This signal was fixed in its most restrictive position and indicated, "proceed preparing to stop at next signal." It served as the distant signal to manually operated lower quadrants at the crossing of D&H and Rutland. *Brian Solomon*

In early British practice all signals were controlled by a signalman. Originally signals displayed only two aspects and each had a specific indication. "Danger" indicated stop, while "Safety" meant it was safe to proceed. Trains approached signals prepared to stop and only when it was determined that a signal displayed "Safety" could it proceed.

This system was adequate when trains stopped at every station along the line since the delays resulting from approaching station signals were of little consequence. However, with the need to run nonstop trains it became necessary to expedite train movements, and the requirement to slow for each signal resulted in undesirable delays.

To keep trains moving, British signaling developed a system of home and distant signals, and a caution aspect/indication was introduced to provide advance warning. When the home displayed "Stop," the distant displayed "Caution," and when the home displayed "Safety," the distant did as well. Significantly, the distant signal was positioned far enough from the home signal so when it displayed "Caution" a train crew had adequate braking distance to stop short of the home signal.

In many instances both home and distant signals were lower-quadrant semaphores. Methods were developed to clearly distinguish home and distant signals arms so there could be no confusion between "Caution" and "Stop" aspects.

The concept of using cautionary aspects gradually grew more complicated as railroads needed to give more specific instructions to train crews. Most of the complexity in advanced signal aspects and indications stems from varying degrees and interpretations of cautionary aspects, located between the need for an absolute "Stop" and an unqualified, safe "Proceed," as well as a desire to provide additional information to the train crew.

Block Versus Junction Signals

Block signals were used to separate train movements on the same track. The home signal was displayed at the entrance to the block. The distant signal aspect was based on the aspect of the home signal at the entrance to the block in advance (ahead) of the train. On single track, block signals were necessary to prevent head-on collisions as well as protect following moves, while on directional double-track lines, block signals were strictly to protect following moves.

Traditionally, in block territory signals didn't grant operating authority to trains but rather were used to provide added safety by ensuring a safe separation

American Signaling Basics 13

between trains. Operating authority was granted by some other established means. In North America authority to use the track was provided by a detailed hierarchy of timetable and train orders. Employee timetables offered specific instructions, which could be amended by train orders issued by centralized operating officials. While this system offered both safety and flexibility, it was subject to interpretation, understanding, and compliance by railroad crews, so human error could (and did) result in accidents.

◉ Written train orders were an integral part of daily operations for more than 150 years. Long Island Rail Road was among the last lines to use this traditional system of authorizing train movements. The operator on the steps at PD Tower holds train order "hoops" used to deliver orders to crews of moving trains. The signal at left has a red light that flashed in conjunction with a "stop" aspect (three lights in a horizontal row) to indicate that a train needed to collect orders. *Patrick Yough*

◉ Train orders were a standard means for providing and amending track authority. A train dispatcher issued orders by telegraph or telephone to an operator who copied them to paper and delivered them to operating crews. On January 29, 1954, a westward Canadian Pacific freight approaches the tower at Lenoxville, Quebec, to take orders from the operator. The tower was located where CP crossed Canadian National's former Grand Trunk route from Portland, Maine, to Montreal. *Jim Shaughnessy*

Manual Block

In a block system, a line was separated into defined segments (blocks) each protected by signals at each end. Originally all block systems were manual block, which required signalmen at each end to communicate with one another regarding the condition of the line before operating signals to allow trains into and out of adjacent blocks. Since all signals in a manual block system were controlled by signalmen, the home and distant system was often applied.

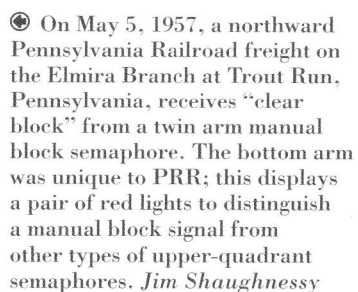

◉ On May 5, 1957, a northward Pennsylvania Railroad freight on the Elmira Branch at Trout Run, Pennsylvania, receives "clear block" from a twin arm manual block semaphore. The bottom arm was unique to PRR; this displays a pair of red lights to distinguish a manual block signal from other types of upper-quadrant semaphores. *Jim Shaughnessy*

◉ Rolling through a late-season snow squall, Pennsylvania Railroad M1A 4-8-2 6734 approaches a manual block signal displaying "clear block" on the Elmira Branch. On the PRR, an upper-quadrant semaphore with two red lights below blade on the right side of the mast and without a number plate distinguished a manual block semaphore from other signals. The pair of red lights could be displayed either with or without a second semaphore arm. *Jim Shaughnessy*

American Signaling Basics **15**

Conrail's western-most semaphore on the former Erie Buffalo Line was signal 356.2B near Dalton, New York. To the west color light and search light signals had replaced the old order. The code lines adjacent to the track were key to signal operation and conveyed vital information including block occupancy. When Conrail replaced semaphores with a modern system in the early 1990s it also removed the traditional code lines. *Brian Solomon*

Signalmen communicated with one another using a telegraph (or in later years, telephone). Specific coded instructions were clearly defined by railroad rules to prevent misunderstanding. An advancement called controlled manual block offered greater protection by using track circuits and relay locks to prevent signalman from making mistakes. By World War I, various types of manual block were widely used, and there was nearly 60,000 miles of railroad under control of manual block in the USA.

Automatic Block

The invention of automatic block was an American innovation made possible by electrically operated signals actuated by electric track circuits that detected the presence of trains or track defects. Railroads first experimented with automatic block signal systems (ABS) in place of manual block in the mid-1870s. An obvious advantage to ABS is that it doesn't require signalmen to operate each and every signal, and thereby lowered operating costs for individual blocks.

Origins of the Approach Aspect

With the ABS, greater capacity was afforded by shortening the length of block sections. However, it was of paramount importance to ensure adequate stopping distance between distant and home signals. The logical and most efficient means of doing this was to combine home and distant signal arms on the same mast. With two-position signals, the top blade/head served the home signal, while the bottom blade/head served as the distant signal (and reflected the condition of the next home signal). With this arrangement each fixed line-side signal could now give a third aspect/indication: "Proceed with caution, prepared to stop at next signal." Because this indicated that the block was clear, and the next signal was at "Stop," it was distinct from "Caution," and later it was named "Approach." It became one of the most common standard aspects/indications.

Permissive Manual Blocks

Another specialized, cautionary aspect/indication was used by only a few railroads for manual block service, where it was desired to keep traffic moving into an occupied block. A permissive indication conditionally allowed trains to follow one another in a block section, advantageous on lines handling heavy freights.

The "Permissive" indication shared similarities with the "Caution" displayed by distant signals and "Stop and proceed" used in ABS service, but had its own distinctive set of conditions. This instructed a train crew to "Proceed—prepared to stop short of obstruction in block." In other words, the block is already occupied, so be aware there is a train ahead. The permissive indication was useful where a helper locomotive might need to follow a train on a long grade, or where two or more slow freights were ascending a grade one right after the other.

Most railroads prohibited passenger trains from accepting permissive indications, thus leading to another important distinction between this indication and other cautionary indications: it was train-type dependent.

16   Chapter 1

Conrail's former Erie Railroad Style S semaphore displays "Approach." During the early years of the twentieth century, signaling proponents variously advocated the advantages of position signals versus light signals. Among the advantages of a traditional semaphore was that its day aspects were unlikely to be confused by individuals suffering from color blindness. *Brian Solomon*

The "Permissive" indication was used by several large railroads, notably the Pennsylvania and Baltimore & Ohio, and was among the reasons these railroads developed their more elaborate position-light/color position light fixed signaling hardware (see Chapter 6). It is important to understand the difference between a "Permissive" indication and a permissive signal—fixed hardware (such as an ABS signal with a pointed blade) that allows a train to continue when displaying its most restrictive aspect.

Three-position Signals

General introduction of the three-position semaphore simplified application of "Approach," since these signals could display three distinct aspects with a single arm. The three basic indications—Stop, Approach, Proceed—became the root for most signaling indications applied to North American signaling schemes, both for ABS and controlled/interlocking signaling arrangements. While combinations of signal heads allowed for a great variety of different cautionary aspects, many of these were for use as diverging signals at junctions.

By 1908, the three-position semaphore was adopted as the preferred standard signal. Despite its advantages, many railroads continued to use, adapt, and install the older two-position style of signals. This produced philosophical differences between two- and three-aspect signals that continued to shape signaling practice for decades. As standard aspects/indications were refined for general and unified applications, both aspects displayed by two-position and three-position types of hardware needed to be accommodated, while standardized indications and rules were based on the progression of three-position semaphore aspects.

Interlocking Aspects

The need for complex signaling at junctions also resulted in distinct philosophies in the ways indications were defined. Signaling was further complicated when technology developed to allow the combining of block and interlocking indications in order to enable trains to follow one another closely, one after the other, through elaborate junctions.

American Signaling Basics

In two-position signaling, junctions were governed by route-specific aspects, where the placement of individual signal blades indicated which route was lined (set) for a train. In the simplest situation, the top signal arm governed movements on the primary route and the bottom arm the diverging route.

The advent of three-position semaphores allowed Pennsylvania Railroad (PRR) to devise an advanced system of speed-specific aspects. Each tier of signal arms represented predefined maximum safe speed for a diverging route: the top arm governed the normal route, the middle arm a medium route, and the bottom arm the lowest speed route. (Generally, only the two lower arms were used for diverging routes.)

Standard signaling codes were adapted from PRR's speed signal philosophy, although some railroads applied older route-signaling guidelines to the new three-position semaphore aspects/indications. In most instances, speed-signaling indications only governed the speed within interlocking limits (see Chapter 2).

What has caused confusion when comparing signaling schemes is that the terms used to describe speeds evolved over time. Furthermore, the specifics of named speeds were intended only as guidelines to railroads, which could assign specific speed values to named speeds to suit their requirements. In the early days of speed signaling, terms such as Limited Speed and Restricted Speed were used in a general sense. So, in the early twentieth century "Limited Speed" meant a cautionary speed (something less than full line speed), while "Restricted Speed" meant a speed slower than limited speed (often half of normal speed).

During development of the standard Codes these speeds were changed and refined to give more specific meanings; the terms medium speed and slow speed became new standards, while later limited speed was redefined, and restricted speed was given a new meaning altogether. (See Chapter 2.)

A westward CSX empty hopper train at dawn works the former Chesapeake & Ohio Kanawha Subdivision in St. Albans, West Virginia, on December 26, 2004. C&O used long-reach cantilever signal gantries to arrange color light signal heads near the tracks that they governed. In recent years, CSX has been replacing C&O's characteristic signal gantries and old US&S signals with standard types of signal masts. *Scott Lothes*

On the evening of November 6, 2010, venerable Union Switch & Signal Style T-2 upper quadrant semaphores protect the former Santa Fe main line timetable west of Colmor, New Mexico. *John Ryan*

Day and Night; Color Signals

Another of the early twentieth century philosophical debates was regarding the need for different aspects in day and night and the colors used for night aspects. Traditionally, daytime signaling relied on the semaphore arms' position to display distinct aspects, while night aspects used colored lenses (known as spectacles) lit from behind by an oil lamp. Some signal engineers desired consistency between day and night aspects and were unsatisfied by the need for engine crews to memorize two sets of signal aspects.

The more serious philosophical difference stemmed from the colors displayed and the meanings assigned to them. Colors used by fixed signal hardware had evolved from colors assigned to hand flag and lanterns—also used for train movements. Traditional British practice had used red for "Danger," green for "Caution," and white for "Safety/Proceed." However, in late nineteenth century British practice the modern color progression was introduced: red for "Danger," yellow for "Caution," and green for "Proceed." Much later, this arrangement was adopted for highway signaling (as well as motorsports), and now the red, yellow, green (R-Y-G) progression is so universally accepted by both railroad and highway signals that it seems bizarre this wasn't always the standard for railway use.

While British railways had largely abandoned the red, green, white (R-G-W) standard by 1890, American railways were slower to universally adopt the new arrangement. Where some progressive lines, such as the New Haven Railroad, were quick to follow Britain's lead, many railroads, including Pennsylvania Railroad and New York Central's Lines West clung to the old standard for decades. There were nearly three decades of overlapping practices before the R-G-W arrangement was totally phased out.

A common pattern resulted in lines changing to R-Y-G as they adopted three-position signaling, yet some railroads continued to use R-G-W with modern hardware, and R-Y-G wasn't universally adopted until after 1917.

American Signaling Basics

American Railway Association
By the early twentieth century, American railroads recognized the need to minimize potential dangers stemming from the inconsistent rules and contradictory practices of different companies. Railroads joined forces, creating voluntary associations that aimed to draft and recommend standard codes of operating rules, including those for line-side signaling practices.

The American Railway Association (ARA) was one of approximately twenty railway associations in place by the early twentieth century, but was by far the most influential. In 1905, it reported that its members

Although several manufacturers sold signal equipment, semaphore blades largely conformed to standard patterns. This diagram shows the standards for a three-position semaphore spectacle. Published in the American Railway Association book *American Railway Signaling Principles and Practices*, Solomon collection

FIG. 119. "CLEAR" INDICATED BY GREEN LIGHT.

20   Chapter 1

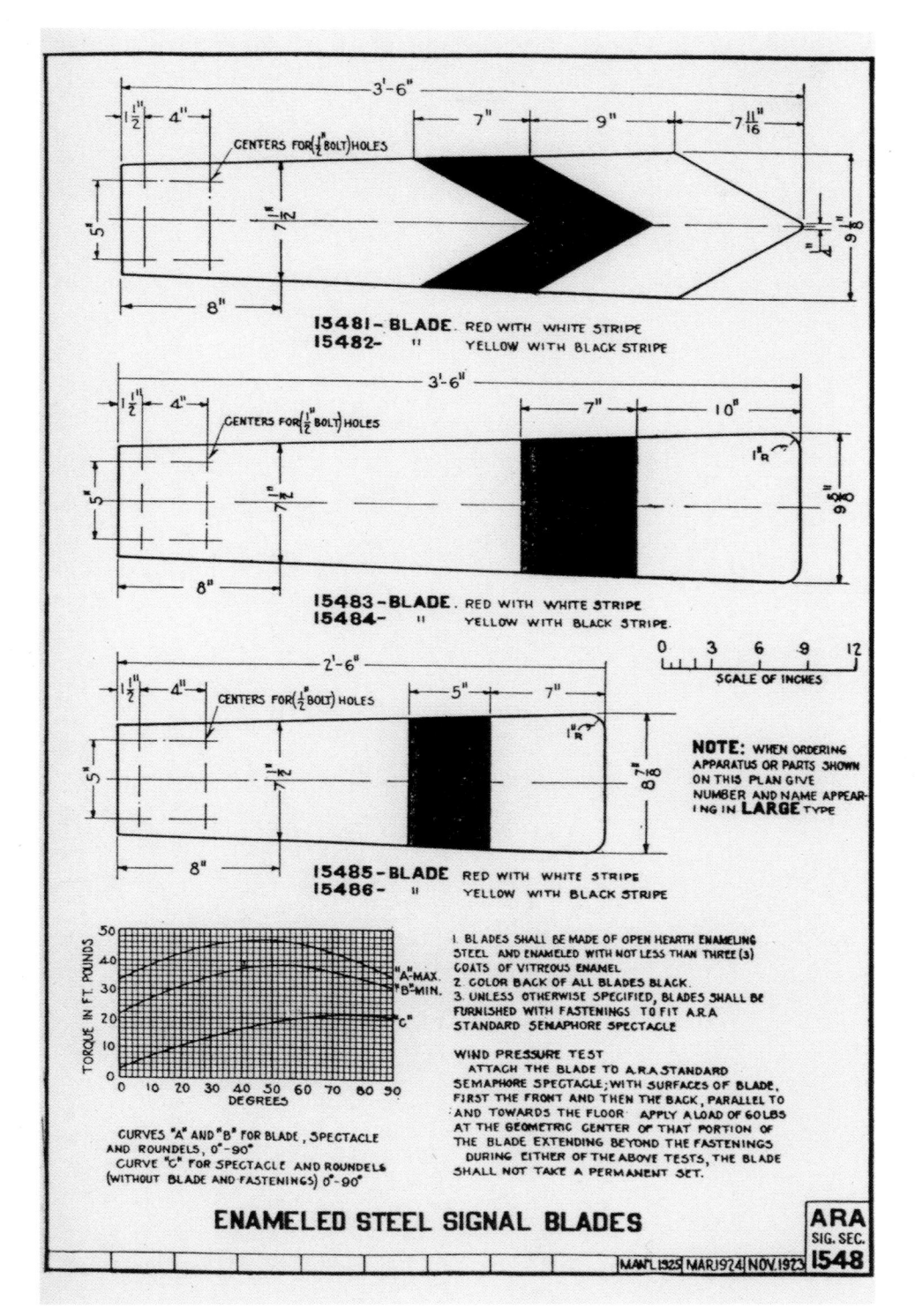

Standard patterns for enameled steel semaphore blades. By 1925, most railroads used either red or yellow blades with stripes or chevrons as shown. Many railroads used blades with pointed ends to distinguish automatic block signals that displayed "stop and proceed" in the horizontal position from signals with a blunt-end blade that displayed "stop." *American Railway Signaling Principles and Practices*, Solomon collection

consisted of 220 railway companies operating in the United States, Canada, and Mexico, which represented more than 220,000 route miles.

The ARA had roots dating back as far as 1872 and included the influential group known as The General Time Convention, which in 1883 established the system of Standard Time zones in the United States and Canada. These zones were the antecedent of today's time zones used worldwide. In April 1891, The General Time Convention changed its name to the American

American Signaling Basics 21

Railway Association (ARA), and this organization was the predecessor to the modern Association of American Railroads (AAR).

ARA's stated object was "the discussion and recommendation of methods for the management and operation of American railways. Its actions are only recommended and not binding upon any member."

Furthermore, in regards to signaling rules, many of ARA's early recommendations reflected the wording and interpretation of rules, rather than strict requirements for implementing hardware. Later its recommendations were expanded to cover specifications of many standard types of signaling equipment, including the shape and dimensions for semaphore blades.

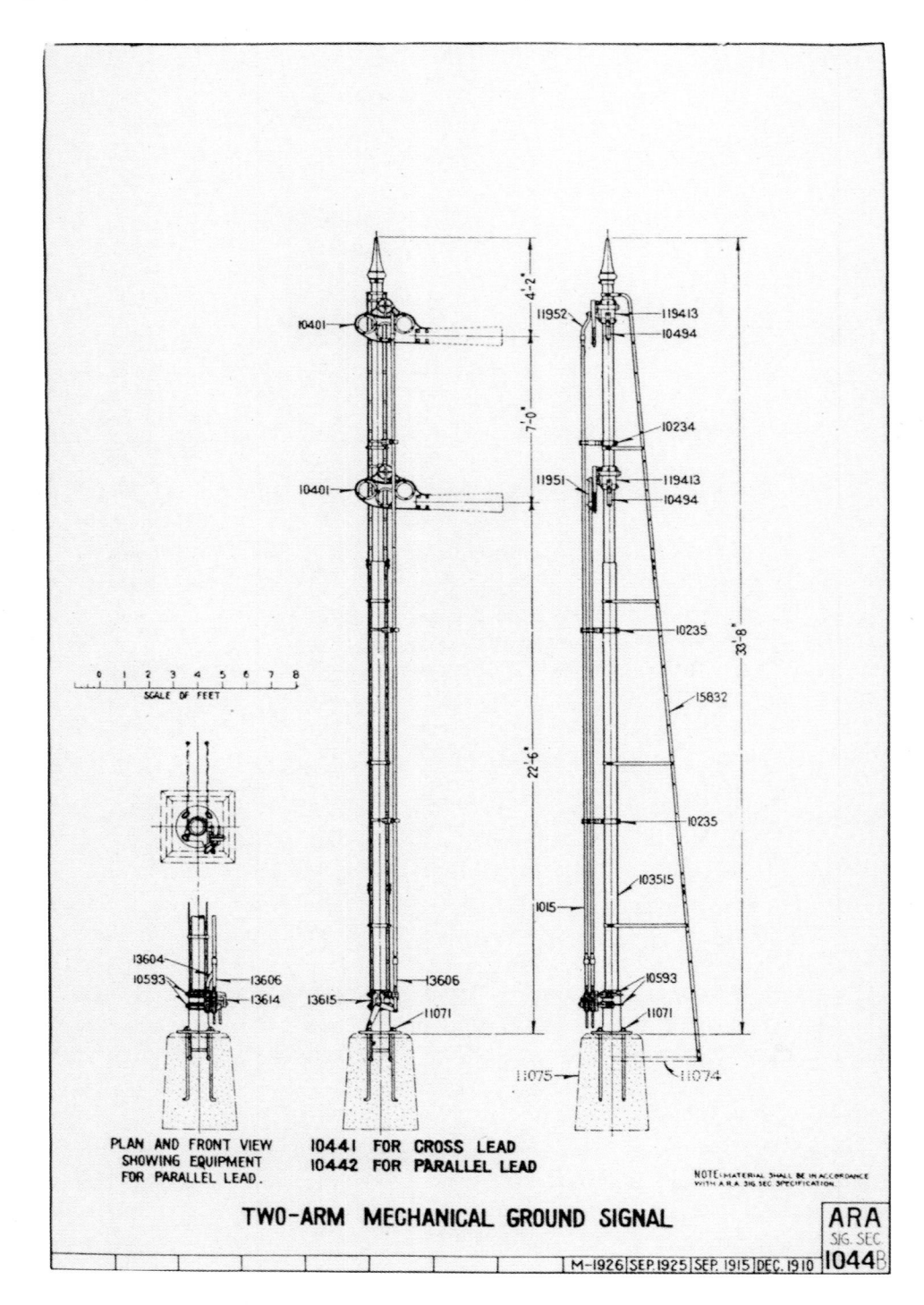

A standard pattern for a two-arm semaphore mast as applied to a mechanical signal for interlocking service. *American Railway Signaling Principles and Practices*, Solomon collection

The Standard Code of 1905

In 1905, the ARA published The Standard Code of rules aimed at unifying practices for railway operations. This included rules for hand signals, whistle signals, and bell signals, as well as rules for operations with fixed signaling hardware. At that time, timetable and train order rules represented the most common form of governing train movements. Fixed signal rules included those for train order boards, interlocking signals, and manual block operations. Automatic block signaling was a relatively modern invention and only provided with nominal treatment.

Fixed signals were only part of an overall rules-regime intended to ensure safe and efficient train movements. ARA's Train Rules for Single Track were adopted on April 12, 1899, and amended on April 23, 1902, while rules for double track were adopted on April 23, 1902. Rules for three and four tracks were adopted in April 1905.

Single-track rules included the use of visible signals (meaning flags and lanterns) and specified the applications of certain colors for these tools. The bulk of the rules spelled out operations by timetable and train order.

Among the significant double-track rules were those "governing the movement with the current of traffic on double track by means of block signals." Rule D-251 read, "On portion of the road so specified on the time-table, trains will run with the current of traffic by block signals whose indications will supercede timetable superiority." Even more significant was rule D-261, "On portions of the road so specified on the time-table, trains will run against the current of traffic by block signals, whose indications will supercede timetable superiority and will take the place of train orders."

Rules 251 and 261 offered means for significant operational changes and established the ability of trains to operate by signal indication without the need for written authority. While the wording has evolved over the years, most railroad rulebooks in the twentieth century made use of rules 251 and 261 on double track, and they remain in many rulebooks to the present day. Rule 251 governs directional double track, while 261 territory is what became known as "two main track," where both lines can be used in either direction, a crucial distinction in operating rules. (A main track is the track used for running trains as opposed to a passing siding, yard track, or other subsidiary track.)

The 1905 Standard Code also laid down some fundamentals for automatic block signaling that set important precedents for its later application and development. It defined the automatic block system as "A series of consecutive blocks controlled by block signals operated by electric, pneumatic or other agency, actuated by a train or by certain conditions affecting the use of a block."

It continued to offer these requisites for ABS signaling:

1. Signals of prescribed form, the indications given by not more than three positions; and, in addition, at night by lights of prescribed color.
2. The apparatus so constructed that the failure of any part controlling the Home Block Signal will cause it to indicate—Stop.
3. Signals, if practicable, either over or upon the right of an adjoining track upon which trains are governed by them. For less than three tracks, signals for trains in each direction may be on the same signal mast. (It goes on to define mast as "the upright to which the signals are directly attached").
4. Semaphore arms that govern, displayed to the right of the signal mast as seen from the approaching train.
5. Switches in the main track so connected with the block signals that the Home Block Signal in the direction of approaching trains will indicate Stop when the switch is not set for the main track.
6. Signal connections and operating mechanism so arranged that a Home Block Signal will indicate Stop after [either the head-end, or the rear] of a train shall have passed it."

The Standard Code prescribes the use of a horizontal semaphore blade and red as the color for a Stop signal, and that a Stop signal indicated "Stop" and should be used when a block is not clear. It goes on to name the other two signals' aspects as a "Clear-signal" indicating "Proceed," and a "Caution-signal," indicating "Approach next home signal prepared to stop," but does not assign colors to them; it notes that "Proceed" may be displayed by either a vertical or diagonal blade position, and "Caution" with a diagonal. These specific aspects were left up to the railroad to delineate in its own rulebook. Similar rules were in effect for interlocking signals.

Defining a Modern Code

At the time of the 1905 Standard Code the number of aspects was still essentially limited to the three basics: "Stop," "Caution," and "Proceed."

By 1910, the three-position upper-quadrant semaphore was the standard signal and was used as the essential defining element for aspects. Where colors were used they were to be applied as equivalent to the position offered by the blades. Although R-Y-G was officially recommended as the progression in 1912, the continued proliferation of the older R-G-W standard was among the reasons for the new standard code to base fundamental aspects on semaphore positions rather than colors. Also at that time, color light signals were only in their infancy, and not yet accepted as standard hardware.

In preparation for formulating a new standard code, members of the Railway Signal Association, including key signaling officers from North American railroads, deliberated, discussed, and argued about the finer points of signaling practice in efforts to devise universally applicable standards. Pennsylvania Railroad's A.H. Rudd was one of the most innovative and progressive signaling officials of his day and among the most influential and vocal. His philosophies shaped all American practice, quoted in *The Railway Gazette* for November 21, 1921:

> "A given signal aspect must transmit the same information at all times, at all places and under all conditions, so that driver will know instantly what it means and whether or not it's displayed correct."

Key to this philosophy was the adoption of uniform aspects when devising the three-position semaphore system.

A Chicago & North Western freight passes ABS semaphores with Model 2A mechanism at Knapp, Wisconsin, on July 5, 1990. C&NW used a distinctively shaped semaphore casting and blade that it deemed to be more visible when viewed from a distance. This style of hardware dated from about 1912. *John Leopard*

New York, Westchester & Boston's unusual suspended two-position center-pivot semaphores were an anomaly in twentieth century North American signaling, and were designed to afford maximum clearance from the high-voltage catenary. They were installed by Union Switch & Signal under the supervision of New Haven signal engineer John Roberts. This view shows North Avenue in New Rochelle, New York, shortly after the railroad was completed in 1912. *Courtesy Robert A. Bang, John Tolley Archive*

Philosophical Differences

Despite guidelines of standard codes, incongruities remained in both hardware styles and signal aspects and indications as a result of continuing philosophical differences: 2-position versus 3-position signals, position aspects versus light aspects, day and night aspects, etc. These differences, combined with the need to reconcile common aspects between interlocking, manual block, automatic block, and train order signals, resulted in a great variety of signaling schemes with different aspects and indications in individual railroad rulebooks.

Further complicating standardized aspects was rapidly evolving signal hardware. Electric lights came of age during the World War I era, and by the mid-1920s these had largely supplanted semaphores as the preferred type of hardware for new installations. While the indications for electric light signals followed the progression offered by the standard code, the variety of new hardware and new types of signaling systems produced many more new aspects.

Adding to the variety were well-meant efforts to reconcile day and night aspects that resulted in

A Reading Company Budd rail diesel car pauses at Quakertown, Pennsylvania, on its run from Bethlehem to Philadelphia in September 1963. Reading was among railroads that used an inverted crescent-shaped blade for train order signals. It was crucial to make train order signals distinctive because such signals did not provide information on track conditions and were only used to alert train crews when they were to receive orders. *Richard Jay Solomon*

invention of position light and color position light signals. In theory, these new systems offered simplified solutions and were intended to limit the number of aspects. This goal might have been achieved if either system had been universally adopted, but instead the opposite occurred. And so position light/color position light signals added to the growing number of aspects used by American railroads.

By the late 1930s, railroads were using a dizzying number of aspects. But, the situation wasn't as chaotic as it might seem. To combat confusion, most railroads adhered to the spirit of indication progression illustrated by the standard codes. Although individual aspects varied with type of hardware, the progression from most restrictive to least restrictive and respective specific indications followed the standard logic and common phraseology. (In other words, while the signal aspects looked different, they conveyed standard instructions.)

Another important point: despite the variety between different railroads, traditionally most train crews and signalmen only needed to be familiar with the specific aspects, indications, and rules that applied to their particular railroad or operation. For the most part, the variations used by other lines didn't affect them. The situation became muddled and more complex as railroads began to merge from the 1960s onward.

Signal Variety

Historically, railroads were dominated by strong-minded personalities who had developed individualist practices in a variety of areas and were reinforced by competing independent companies. Since each railroad was different, every company developed signaling requirements for its traffic requirements, taking into consideration the effects of line profiles and operating styles.

A railroad with a lightly traveled single-track line had considerably different signaling needs than a heavily traveled multiple-track route serving complex junctions and busy terminals. Where the former may have only required basic block protection, the latter had a need for complex, multiple-aspect speed signaling.

High costs of signaling installations combined with the great durability of hardware meant that once a railroad invested in signaling infrastructure it wasn't inclined to make changes to the system, except where investment would clearly improve profits. Railroads that made an early investment in signaling often retained older equipment styles rather than replace signaling to satisfy philosophical desires for standardization.

Central Railroad of New Jersey 2-8-2 923 with 133 empty coal hoppers in tow blasts under a multiple-track signal bridge supporting lower-quadrant semaphores at Cranford, New Jersey. The blunt-ended arms are home signals controlled by the tower seen in the background to the left on the far side of the train. Automatic block signals, such as those governing the movement of this freight, feature the common lower-quadrant automatic block arrangement with pointed-end home arms above fishtail-end distant arms. *Donald W. Furler*

American Signaling Basics 27

Reinforcing this philosophy was the desire to maintain aspect/hardware consistency on individual lines. A transition period from one style of hardware to another, or a significant change to rules, might lead to confusion, and confusing signal aspects was a recipe for disaster.

Early to embrace the electric two-position, lower-quadrant semaphore, Southern Pacific continued to install this type of hardware to maintain consistency for decades after more advanced signals were available. Even more extreme was Philadelphia & Reading, which continued to install Hall enclosed disc signals as late as 1914 (see Chapter 3).

Standard Code of 1912

In 1912, after years of discussion, the American Railway Association and Railway Signal Association agreed to a practical and limited number of aspects based on daytime three-position semaphore positions. Provisions for equivalent aspects were also included for two-position, lower-quadrant signaling. While ARA had advised the R-Y-G color progression since 1896, in the 1912 codebook this arrangement was more strongly encouraged.

Significantly, the code offered three signaling schemes (all based on the standard three-position semaphore aspects) with which railroads could base their rulebooks. Each scheme was based on the number of semaphore arms employed:

Scheme one was the most basic, based on single-arm signals to provide the three most common aspects: horizontal blade indicating "Stop"; 45-degree blade indicating "Proceed With Caution"; and an upright (vertical blade) indicating "Proceed."

Scheme two used two arm signals and offered simple speed signaling with five indications and eight aspects. When a signal scheme uses multiple blades and/or when ground level signals (known as dwarfs) are used, more than one aspect may be used for the same indication. "Stop" for example, may be displayed by either one horizontal arm or two, or a dwarf semaphore displaying a horizontal. Five of the eight aspects used twin-arm signals; the top arm signified a normal speed route, while the lower arm was used for routes less than normal speed (usually diverging from the main route) and the actual speeds were left up to the railroad.

Aspects included: horizontal blade over a 45-degree blade indicated "Proceed at low speed" (in other words proceed on a diverging

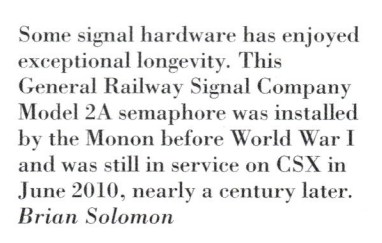

Some signal hardware has enjoyed exceptional longevity. This General Railway Signal Company Model 2A semaphore was installed by the Monon before World War I and was still in service on CSX in June 2010, nearly a century later. *Brian Solomon*

28 Chapter 1

A view made shortly after sunrise on July 17, 2008, shows Union Switch & Signal searchlights at the west end of Alford Siding (Alford, Oregon) on Union Pacific's former Southern Pacific Cascade Route. Southern Pacific designated all of its lines on an east–west axis. Regardless of compass direction, the direction of travel toward its San Francisco headquarters was always "west." As a result, SP's Cascade Route was viewed as an east–west operation despite its largely north–south alignment. *Scott Lothes*

slow speed route); horizontal over a vertical indicated "Proceed at medium speed"; and vertical blade over a horizontal blade could be used for "Proceed" (on normal speed route) and thus shared this indication with a single vertical arm.

Scheme three followed a similar progression using three arm signals for speed signaling. This featured eight indications and twenty aspects. One-, two-, and three-arm tall signals and dwarfs all displayed "Stop," so there were four aspects for "Stop" covering all combinations of semaphore arms, and in all the aspects arms were displayed horizontally. Three additional indications were: "Proceed with caution on low speed route"; "Proceed with caution on medium speed route"; and "Reduce to medium speed." This scheme enabled combining interlocking and automatic block aspects, while allowing considerable signaling flexibility for complex junctions where track capacity was often pushed to its practical limits.

In 1928 the ARA restandardized the standard code, introducing standard names for aspects and revised indications and rules. Changes covered provisions for new types of light signals including position lights and color position light hardware. In 1938 and again in 1949, the Association of American Railroads (successor to the ARA) made further revisions to its signal code. The rule numbers, aspects, and indications from this period are similar to those still in use today, although continued refinement has resulted in a great number of changes.

Block Signals in the Standard Code of 1949

By this time all railroads were using the R-Y-G progression and semaphore positions equated with their corresponding night color aspects, largely the same as used by various types of color light hardware. The

American Signaling Basics 29

code also accommodated equivalent aspects' displays for position light and color position light systems (see Chapter 6).

The basic indications "Stop" and "Proceed" had simple rules, but the multitude of cautionary aspects required detailed instructions in the rules. Most railroads adopted only a selection of cautionary aspects/indications for their specific signaling requirements. However, a few lines such as New York Central filled their rulebooks with a great number of aspects.

The basic cautionary aspect displayed a 45-degree diagonal blade, by now formally equated with a yellow light and named "Approach," which indicated "proceed in accordance with operating rules," and so carried a specific restriction from a full "Proceed." As applied to automatic block and interlocking signals, "Approach" involved a more defined rule and application than the older instruction "proceed with caution" (see rule 285 page 51). Yet, the 45-degree blade and/or yellow light could also be applied as a cautionary signal for manual block and for train order signal situations, provided there were clear distinguishing features.

Two-Block, Three-Aspect Signaling

The majority of automatic block signaling in North America used two-block protection for following movements, where a "Clear" aspect indicated "Proceed" and signified that the next two blocks were clear. "Approach" indicated one block was clear, and a train should be prepared to stop at the next signal.

Essential to the safe operation of two-block arrangements was that the distance between block signals provided sufficient braking distance for all trains operating at the highest prescribed line speed. When a train passed a signal displaying "Approach" there must be no question it can come to a safe stop short of the next block signal.

Safe signal spacing depended on line profile (gradient and curvature), operating line speed, maximum train weights, and other considerations that affected braking distances. Among block length considerations were signal sighting requirements and restrictions imposed by heavy infrastructure such as bridges, tunnels, and highway grade crossings. To help ensure safe operation, a factor of safety was considered when calculating braking distances.

Longer blocks offered greater braking distances, but longer blocks also reduced line capacity, so signal engineers need to balance the necessities of safe operation with traffic demands. When traffic mandated shorter block length than safe operation allowed, another solution was needed.

Three-Block, Four-Aspect Signaling and "Advance Approach"

The desire to safely operate trains at higher speeds required either more effective braking systems or alterations to the signaling system. To accommodate greater braking distance, blocks could be lengthened. Since this limited line capacity, a compromise resulted in the introduction of three-block, four-aspect signaling.

Under this scheme, it is assumed that trains may require two blocks to come to safe stop and that one block no longer provided adequate stopping distance. As a result, an additional cautionary aspect was needed to inform the train crew that the next signal displayed "Approach" and that the signal after that displayed "Stop" (thus providing two blocks' protection). Although this straightforward requirement should have a simple solution, perhaps no other aspect has resulted in as much controversy and various interpretations.

Complicating the application of the fourth block signal aspect are the implications imposed by the approach to junctions (including passing sidings protected by controlled/absolute signals) and speeds through those junctions. Further complications are related to the type of hardware employed. The result was a variety of fourth aspects.

When a railroad is pressed to capacity, many solutions become impractical since they might obviate the advantages of three-block protection.

In three-block ABS, a common aspect progression from most restrictive to least restrictive is as follows: "Stop/Stop and Proceed," "Approach," "Advance Approach," and finally "Clear."

Advance Approach (Rule 282A) indicated "Proceed preparing to stop at second signal," with a further instruction, "Trains exceeding medium speed must at once reduce to that speed." Under this definition, the signal could be used to ensure adequate braking distance both in three-block ABS territory and in a three-block approach to an interlocking.

This was often displayed using a pair of 45-degree blades (and/or yellow lights), one over the other (where three blades/heads are used, a horizontal blade and/or red light may be at the lowest position). One reason offered for the name "Advance Approach" instead of "Approach Approach" was because when crews called

In the 1920s, Denver Rio Grande & Western adopted color light signals using a vertical pattern and a single large shade to improve sighting of signal lights in bright sun. Multiple diverging routes required three heads; this westward absolute signal was located at Soldier Summit, Utah, where a single track faced the beginning of two-main tracks (double track where trains could use either track on signal indication), and a dispatcher controlled siding. *J. D. Schmid*

out the signal in the locomotive cab there was a risk that it may sound as if "Approach" was simply repeated, which could be potentially confusing.

Over the years there have been different philosophies for the most appropriate aspect used to indicate when the second signal displays "Stop." An alternative to "Advance Approach" was the application of "Approach Medium"—displayed with a vertical blade (and/or green light) over 45-degree blade (and/or yellow light), as defined in Chapter 2. This aspect offered a logical progression for some railroads, such as Baltimore & Ohio, but also presented some incongruous situations, leading to many railroads preferring "Advance Approach."

In New York Central's rulebook (revised in April 1949), Rule 282A (Advance Approach) indicated "proceed preparing to stop at second signal. Trains exceeding limited speed must at once reduce to that speed. Reduction to limited speed must commence before passing signal and be completed before accepting a more favorable indication."

Four-color light aspects were given for this indication, as displayed by two- and three-light interlocking signals, two-light ABS signals, and two-light dwarf signals. All four aspects were logical variations of yellow over yellow. Central used "Advance Approach" without worrying whether "Approach Medium" would also provide a safe system. In fact, on Central, "Advance Approach" allowed crews to approach the next signal faster than if an "Approach Medium" were displayed.

In a color light system, a single flashing yellow light has also been used in place of double yellow. This aspect has the cost advantage of requiring only one signal head to display all four aspects. Santa Fe and Southern Pacific were among the proponents of this scheme.

Philosophical objections to using the yellow over yellow aspect for Advance Approach stem from this aspect also being applied by other signaling schemes for slower indications. It has also been used to display "Approach Slow," (see Chapter 2—Interlocking Aspects), while railroads that use route signaling, such as Southern Pacific, assigned yellow over yellow for "Approach Diverging" (SP Rule 233: "Proceed prepared to advance on diverging route at next signal at prescribed speed through turnout").

Most semaphores in automatic block service were wired in the "normal clear" arrangement, whereby the signal displayed clear until the track circuit was shunted (by a train, the lining of a switch, or a fault). North of Linden, Indiana, a train passing a Model 2A semaphore shunts the track circuit, allowing the signal arm to drop by gravity from the vertical position to the horizontal. Pointed blades and masts with number plates meant that these ABS signals displayed "Stop and Proceed" in the horizontal position. *Chris Guss*

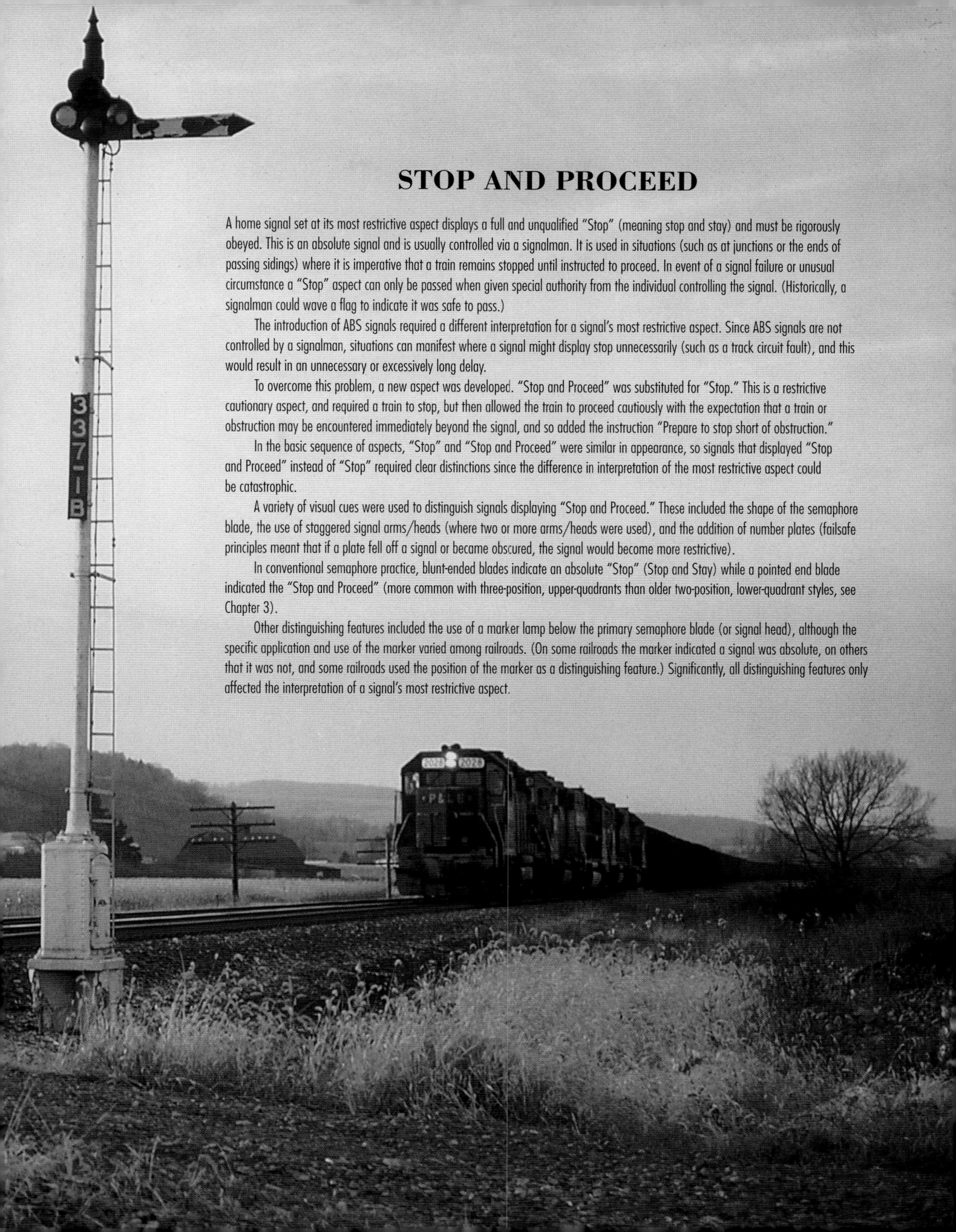

STOP AND PROCEED

A home signal set at its most restrictive aspect displays a full and unqualified "Stop" (meaning stop and stay) and must be rigorously obeyed. This is an absolute signal and is usually controlled via a signalman. It is used in situations (such as at junctions or the ends of passing sidings) where it is imperative that a train remains stopped until instructed to proceed. In event of a signal failure or unusual circumstance a "Stop" aspect can only be passed when given special authority from the individual controlling the signal. (Historically, a signalman could wave a flag to indicate it was safe to pass.)

The introduction of ABS signals required a different interpretation for a signal's most restrictive aspect. Since ABS signals are not controlled by a signalman, situations can manifest where a signal might display stop unnecessarily (such as a track circuit fault), and this would result in an unnecessary or excessively long delay.

To overcome this problem, a new aspect was developed. "Stop and Proceed" was substituted for "Stop." This is a restrictive cautionary aspect, and required a train to stop, but then allowed the train to proceed cautiously with the expectation that a train or obstruction may be encountered immediately beyond the signal, and so added the instruction "Prepare to stop short of obstruction."

In the basic sequence of aspects, "Stop" and "Stop and Proceed" were similar in appearance, so signals that displayed "Stop and Proceed" instead of "Stop" required clear distinctions since the difference in interpretation of the most restrictive aspect could be catastrophic.

A variety of visual cues were used to distinguish signals displaying "Stop and Proceed." These included the shape of the semaphore blade, the use of staggered signal arms/heads (where two or more arms/heads were used), and the addition of number plates (failsafe principles meant that if a plate fell off a signal or became obscured, the signal would become more restrictive).

In conventional semaphore practice, blunt-ended blades indicate an absolute "Stop" (Stop and Stay) while a pointed end blade indicated the "Stop and Proceed" (more common with three-position, upper-quadrants than older two-position, lower-quadrant styles, see Chapter 3).

Other distinguishing features included the use of a marker lamp below the primary semaphore blade (or signal head), although the specific application and use of the marker varied among railroads. (On some railroads the marker indicated a signal was absolute, on others that it was not, and some railroads used the position of the marker as a distinguishing feature.) Significantly, all distinguishing features only affected the interpretation of a signal's most restrictive aspect.

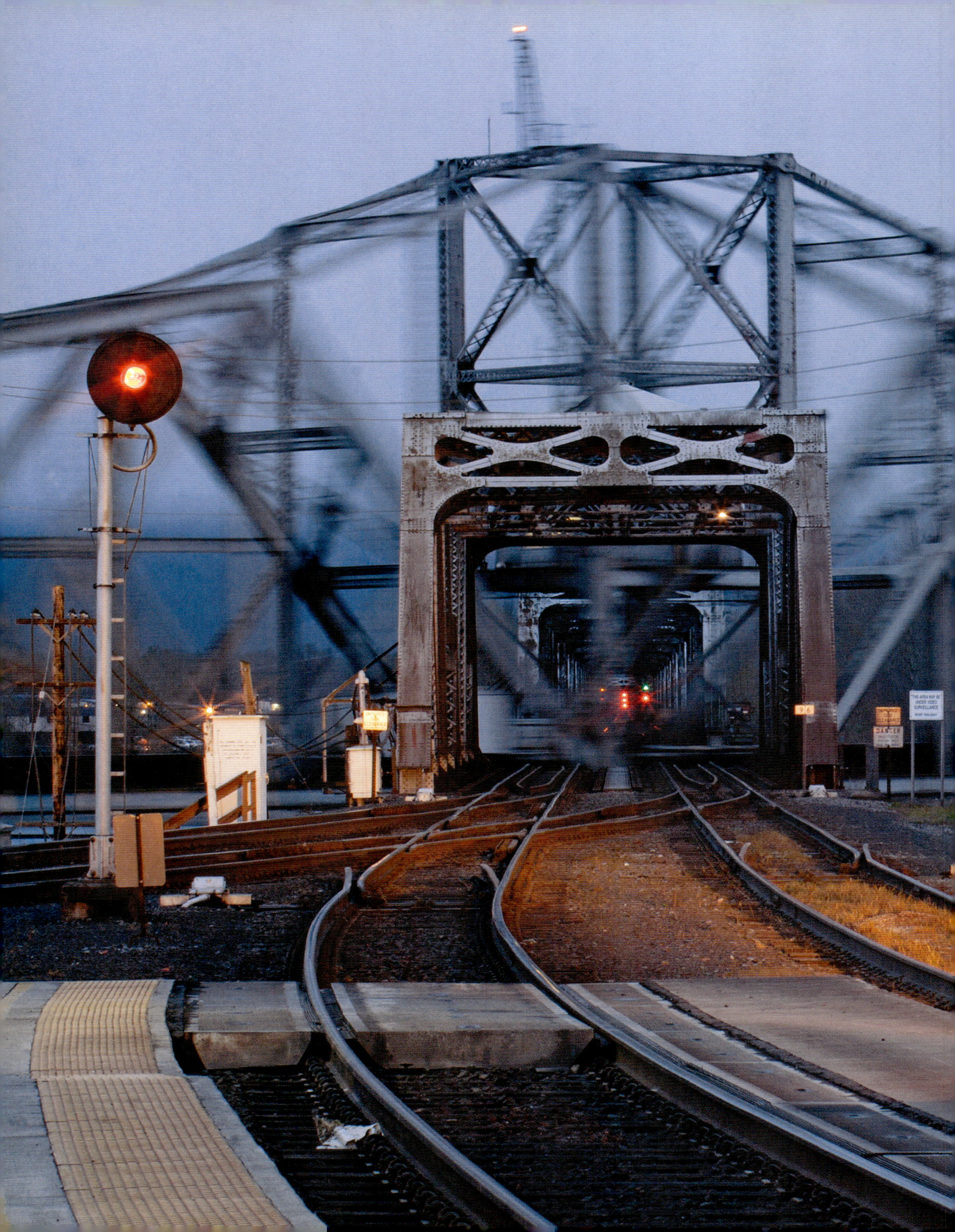
THIS AREA MAY BE
UNDER VIDEO
SURVEILLANCE
DANGER

TOWERS AND INTERLOCKING SIGNALS

2

Junction Signals

The earliest use of signals was at junctions where lines and/or tracks came together. Following some serious accidents, safeguards known as interlockings were developed. Interlocking plants control switches and signals at junctions, crossings, and drawbridges. The primary purpose of an interlocking is to prevent conflicting routes from being authorized and that conditions are safe for trains to pass. Safety checks are in place to ensure that each route is complete (all switches lined and locked for movement on the desired route) and that no conflicting or opposing movement is authorized that would endanger a train's safety before signals can be set for the route.

Interlocking signals were often covered by their own set of rules. A classic definition for interlocking is that used in Erie Railroad's November 30, 1952, Rules of the Operating Department:

> An arrangement of signals and signal appliances so interconnected that their movements succeed each other in proper sequence and for which interlocking rules are in effect. It may be operated manually or automatically...

On March 28, 2008, a Portland & Western freight waits for a clear signal at BNSF Railway's Columbia River drawbridge. This view is looking south from the station in Vancouver, Washington. Interlocking home signals are used at junctions, crossings, and drawbridges where absolute stops are necessary to prevent collisions. Notice the derails beyond the home signals. These provide a greater level of protection for the drawbridge. *Scott Lothes*

35

A modern interpretation is provided in the 2008 Northeast Operating Rules Advisory Committee (NORAC) rules defining interlockings as:

> An interconnection of signals and signal appliances such that their movements must succeed each other in a predetermined sequence, assuring that signals cannot be displayed simultaneously on conflicting routes. Interlocking rules are in effect in an interlocking.

Types of Interlocking Plants

An interlocking can use mechanical, electrical, or a combination of these systems to ensure that switches, signals, and appliances (such as derails, movable frogs, and locking bars) are in their safe and proper positions. In modern times, solid state logic and microprocessors have been employed for interlocking controls, but historically this was done by mechanical means. Advances in electrical and electronic control allowed for vastly larger and more complex control from a single point.

Towers

Historically, interlockings were controlled from a tower, which housed control mechanisms and provided a work space for signal operators. (Railroad philosophy frowned on sharing signal towers with other functions.) In its classic form, a tower offered an elevated view of the interlocking it controlled to allow signalmen to observe the condition of signals and switch points as well as passing trains.

Operator Jeff Varney works Rondout Tower, which protects the crossing of former Milwaukee Road and Elgin, Joliet & Eastern lines, and the junction with the former Milwaukee line to Janesville and Madison. Track switches and signals are set using the CTC panel, while the operator has various means to communicate with railroad personnel. *Chris Guss*

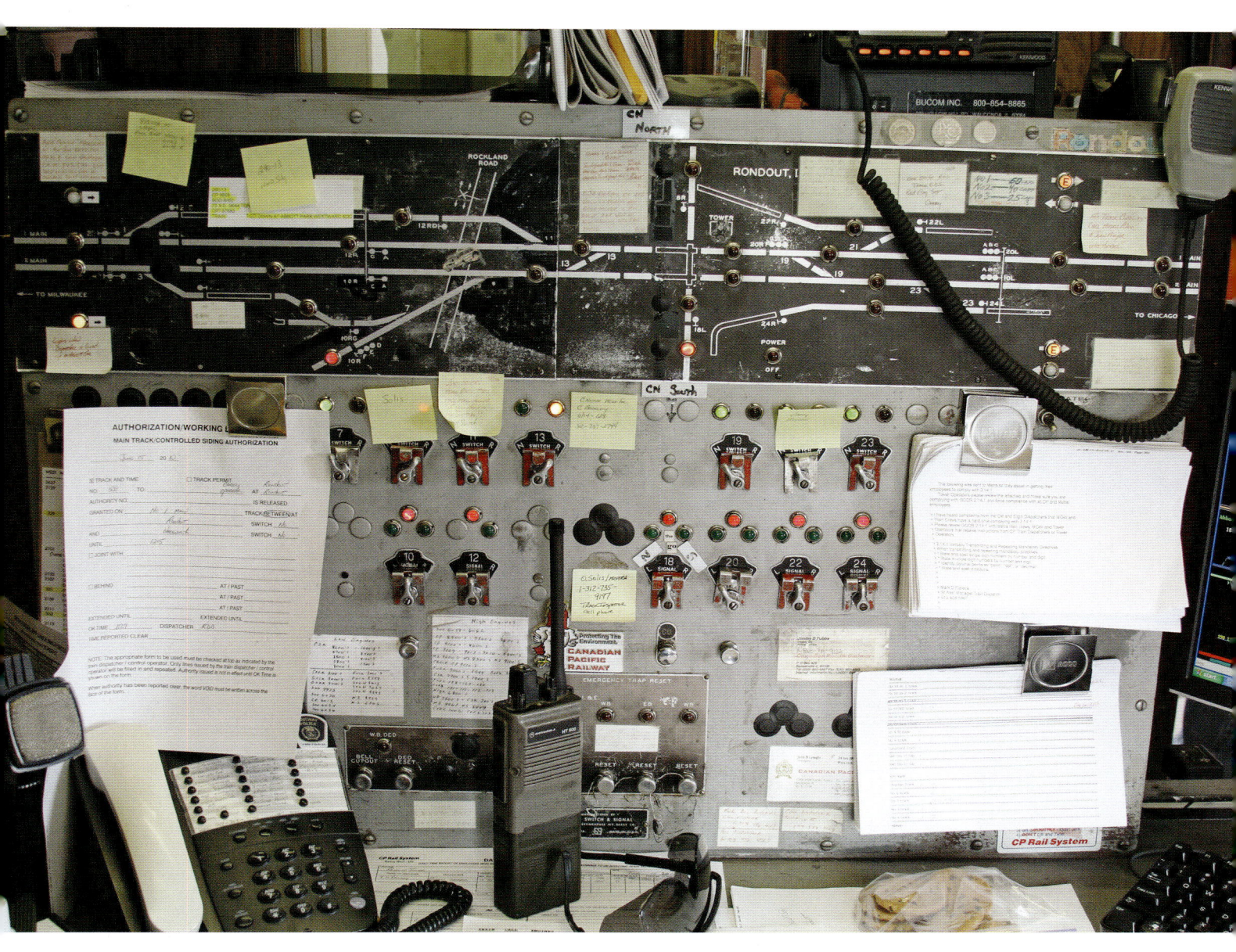

Detailed view of the operator's model board at Canadian Pacific's former Milwaukee Road Rondout Tower, Rondout, Illinois. Advances in electric relay control allowed for a reduction in the size of signal and switch controls and the combining of control functions, while later advances in semi-conductor development and computer controls greatly expanded the scope of control afforded a single operator. *Brian Solomon*

Towers served as railroad nerve centers where skilled signalmen directed train operations. Next to the locomotive cab, it was one of the best places to experience railroading. Bells rang, relays clicked, instructions were received by telegraph or telephone, as men acted to keep the railroad fluid. A busy tower offered intense bursts of activity as signalmen lined and locked routes and set signals by hand to make the way for passing trains.

As technology advanced, the combination of sophisticated tools for controlling interlockings over great distances resulted in a gradual consolidation of signal control to centralized locations. Ultimately, it was no longer necessary to house interlocking controls in line-side locations. Towers, which once dotted the railroad landscape by the thousands, have been in steadily declining numbers for more than 100 years. By 2014, only a handful survive.

TOWER CONSTRUCTION

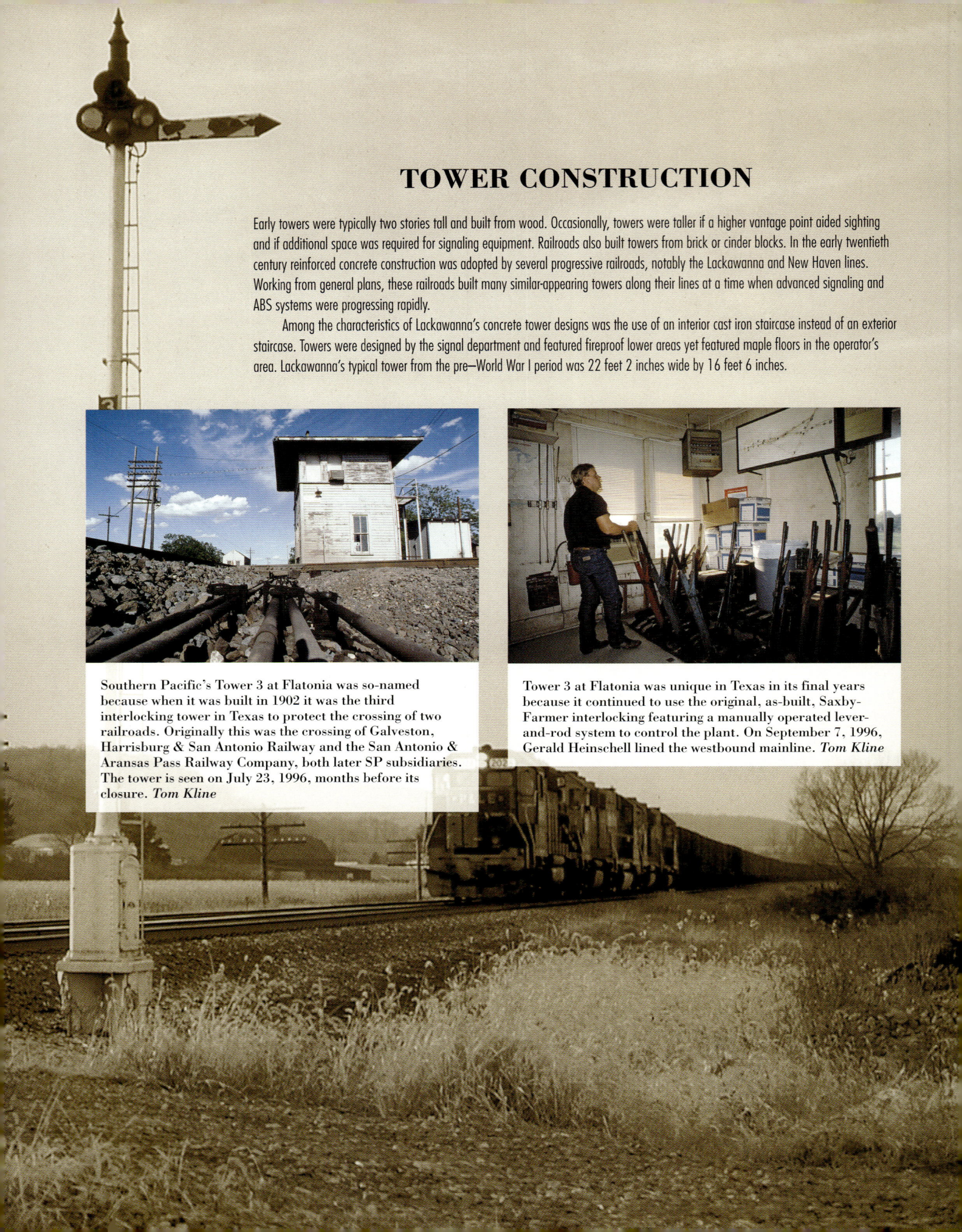

Early towers were typically two stories tall and built from wood. Occasionally, towers were taller if a higher vantage point aided sighting and if additional space was required for signaling equipment. Railroads also built towers from brick or cinder blocks. In the early twentieth century reinforced concrete construction was adopted by several progressive railroads, notably the Lackawanna and New Haven lines. Working from general plans, these railroads built many similar-appearing towers along their lines at a time when advanced signaling and ABS systems were progressing rapidly.

Among the characteristics of Lackawanna's concrete tower designs was the use of an interior cast iron staircase instead of an exterior staircase. Towers were designed by the signal department and featured fireproof lower areas yet featured maple floors in the operator's area. Lackawanna's typical tower from the pre–World War I period was 22 feet 2 inches wide by 16 feet 6 inches.

Southern Pacific's Tower 3 at Flatonia was so-named because when it was built in 1902 it was the third interlocking tower in Texas to protect the crossing of two railroads. Originally this was the crossing of Galveston, Harrisburg & San Antonio Railway and the San Antonio & Aransas Pass Railway Company, both later SP subsidiaries. The tower is seen on July 23, 1996, months before its closure. *Tom Kline*

Tower 3 at Flatonia was unique in Texas in its final years because it continued to use the original, as-built, Saxby-Farmer interlocking featuring a manually operated lever-and-rod system to control the plant. On September 7, 1996, Gerald Heinschell lined the westbound mainline. *Tom Kline*

Interlocking towers controlled an array of track switches, derails, and signals to route and protect trains traveling through their territory. Sitting atop the interlocking machine at Tower 17 in Rosenberg, Texas, are instructions detailing lever combinations needed to route Southern Pacific and Santa Fe trains through the crossing. This 26-lever interlocking tower was built by the SP in 1903 and remained in service until 1996, when it was donated by SP-successor Union Pacific to the Rosenberg Railroad Museum and restored for display. *Tom Kline*

Interlocking Types

Four types of interlockings—all mechanical, electromechanical, electropneumatic, and all electric systems—accounted for the types of control used by most American towers.

The mechanical interlocking was the invention of John Saxby, a foreman with the London, Brighton & South Coast Railway. In 1856, he developed and patented a mechanical lever frame that interlocked the movements of signal and switch levers. In 1863, he went into business with John Farmer to manufacture signal interlocking equipment. Not only were interlocking concepts imported from England, but a great many Saxby & Farmer interlocking mechanisms were built in North America for domestic applications.

The mechanical system featured large levers with direct mechanical linkages to switch points, signals, and other apparatus. Commonly a pipeline network transmitted power to equipment in the field. These were worked manually by able-bodied operators with the strength to move points, which might be located considerable distances from the tower. Semaphores could be operated by either pipe or wire networks.

This mechanical semaphore at 75th Street Tower, Chicago, provides a nice silhouette against a January 2, 1995, morning sky. The 132-lever Saxby & Farmer mechanical interlocking was originally installed in July 1908, by the Federal Signal Company of Troy, New York. Its location at 75th Street is where Chicago Terminal Transfer Railroad crossed Baltimore & Ohio Chicago Terminal, Belt Railway of Chicago, Wabash, and Pennsylvania Railroad's Panhandle line. This junction was completely re-signaled 89 years later by which time it was among the last mechanical plants in the Chicago area. *Brian Solomon*

Towers and Interlocking Signals   **39**

A mechanical upper-quadrant dwarf semaphore at 75th Street Tower, Chicago on January 2, 1995. Installed in 1908, this was still at work in 1995. Imagine the uncountable steam and diesel locomotives that worked their way past this venerable signal over its decades of service. *Brian Solomon*

The interlocking machine was key to fail-safe operation; this used a precision bed of notched metal bars carefully designed to insure that switches, locks, signals and related equipment moved in a safe predetermined order. The machine provided mechanical interference to prevent operators from lining conflicting routes or other unsafe or unauthorized movements.

An advancement of the strictly mechanical interlocking was the electromechanical plant, which relied on the same essential type of mechanical interlocking mechanism but blended mechanical and electric equipment to allow for control of a larger plant and over greater distances. In one of the more common electromechanical arrangements, switches were controlled through mechanical linkages, while signals were operated electrically.

The all-electric interlocking was a further advancement. This still relied on a mechanical interlocking frame but switches, locks, and signals were all operated electrically. This overcame many of the limitations of mechanical operation and allowed for control of an even larger plant. Also an electric plant could be wired so that when a route was locked the power to switch machines was cut to prevent the accidental realignment of points beneath the wheels of a train, which eliminated the need for mechanical locking bars.

Another type was electropneumatic interlocking, which used air-actuated equipment to move switch points, and in some instances signals. A central pneumatic station supplied pressurized air to line-side equipment. Among the advantages of pneumatic control was faster movement of switch points. This was desirable at large terminals with complex trackage and frequent train movements and arrangements. Another advantage was in areas where flooding could be a problem, since pneumatic interlockings are easier to dry out and put back in service after being immersed in water.

These mechanical upper-quadrant semaphores at Brighton Park in Chicago were built to the Loree–Patenall patent of 1903. The non-interlocked level crossing required all trains to stop before being signaled through the junction by semaphore indication. It was among the last crossings in the Chicago area protected by mechanical semaphores, and was finally upgraded in 2007 with modern systems and color light signals. *Brian Solomon*

40   Chapter 2

◉ A quiet morning at CSX's Q Tower at Hardman, West Virginia, on October 15, 1994. This former Baltimore & Ohio electromechanical interlocking, located east of Grafton, West Virginia, on the Mountain Subdivision, used a mechanical pipeline to line switch points and electrical controls to clear signals. *Brian Solomon*

◉ Westward helpers approach CSX's Q Tower at Hardman, West Virginia. Line-side interlocking towers survived on CSX's former Baltimore & Ohio lines decades longer than on other American mainlines. By the time of this image the tower had a reduced role from its heyday and many of the old manual levers were out of service. *Brian Solomon*

Further advancement of electrical technology enabled development of all-relay and finally electronic interlocking systems. Advanced interlocking controls featured smaller control levers and push button controls, while more sophisticated circuitry permitted more advanced routing controls and automatic routing functions. Combining electronic interlocking features with track circuitry and limited release functions enabled interlocking signals to be blended with automatic block functions, which enabled trains to follow one another in rapid succession over complex routes across the plant.

Interlocking Rules and Aspects

In the early days, junctions used simple aspects that simply showed "Proceed" or "Stop," most often with mechanical lower-quadrant semaphores. As interlocking plants grew more complex, route signaling was developed to advise crews on the route(s) they were taking. On some railroads, lower-quadrant signals had as many as five arms to show different routes. Adoption of three-position semaphores limited signals to just three arms, and allowed railroads to adopt standard speed signaling rules.

Interlocking aspects were designed to give crews specific instructions on the maximum safe speed over the route lined through a junction. In addition, some aspects also provided advance warning for conditions imposed by the next signal. Interlocking aspects could be blended with ABS information in order to enable trains to follow in rapid succession over the same route. This is especially important at busy junctions where congestion would result in costly delays.

Generally speaking, interlocking speed signaling indications are only intended to safely govern train speed through interlocking limits and do not apply to line speed beyond the interlocking. Indications have been carefully worded to instruct crews when they are supposed to make reductions in speed and when they can resume normal speed.

Why were such a variety of cautionary interlocking aspects developed? Different speeds required specific train handling instructions to keep traffic moving at the

Towers and Interlocking Signals 41

New York, Westchester & Boston's Columbus Avenue Tower was just completed in this 1912 photograph. This was one of seven electric interlocking plants on NYW&B and featured a Union Switch & Signal Style F electric interlocking machine. NYW&B was a short-lived suburban electric railway; it opened in 1912 and ended operations in 1937. *Courtesy Robert A. Bang, John Tolley Archive*

maximum safe speed and to make the most of track capacity. Trains of different weights and maximum speeds may travel a variety of routes served by the same home signals.

Some of the more complicated aspects, such a "Medium Approach Slow," were primarily used for major junctions or at terminals, to expedite a train facing multiple junctions in a relatively short distance where track capacity is at a premium. An unnecessarily restrictive aspect would constrain track capacity at the very location where capacity was needed most urgently.

42   Chapter 2

The Association of American Railroad's Standard Code of 1949 offered railroads a variety of interlocking aspects to work from. Railroads tended to only adapt those aspects necessary for their specific operations. Yet, occasionally, companies would find it necessary to adopt non-conforming aspects to provide signal protection in unusual circumstances.

Each individual railroad's signal practices dictated the style of hardware and the way aspects were actually displayed. While aspects varied, standardized wording was adapted by individual railroad rulebooks and resulted in only minor variations in individual railroads' indications.

A New Haven Railroad Alco PA approaches Boston's South Station on March 11, 1956. This terminal's large electropneumatic interlocking and lower-quadrant semaphore signaling was installed under the able administration of US&S signaling genius J.P Coleman in 1897–1898. Some of the signals remained in service until South Station was reconfigured in the mid-1980s. *Jim Shaughnessy*

⊕ A Central Railroad of New Jersey Budd-built rail diesel car departs Jersey City on November 29, 1964. Fifty years earlier, CNJ rebuilt its Jersey City terminal with a state-of-the-art Union Switch & Signal electropneumatic system. *Richard Zmijewski*

⊕ Against a backdrop of the Manhattan skyline, Reading's *Crusader* departs Central Railroad of New Jersey's Jersey City terminal for Philadelphia. CNJ's complex plant featured three interlocking towers, which controlled a nine-track throat with four ladder arrangements (two in each direction) that allowed parallel movements for trains to reach platforms. Three-position, upper-quadrant electropneumatic semaphores governed train movements. *Richard Jay Solomon*

44   Chapter 2

The model board in Metro-North's former New Haven Railroad New Haven West Tower shows the track arrangement at its namesake Connecticut station platform area. This photograph was taken on May 10, 2003; the tower has since closed. *Patrick Yough*

Speeds

By 1949, normal speed was defined as the maximum safe speed on a main route. Recommended cautionary speeds that warranted speed signal aspects were: Limited Speed (60 miles per hour), Medium Speed (40 miles per hour), and Slow Speed (20 miles per hour). However, railroads have assigned different numerical values to the named speeds and over the years definitions have been changed to suit individual rulebooks.

For example, the 2008 NORAC definitions are more restrictive with each rule prefaced by "not exceeding": Limited Speed is listed as 45 miles per hour for passenger, 40 miles per hour for freight; Medium Speed 30 miles per hour; and Slow Speed 15 miles per hour.

The AAR rules have standard numbers that progress from least restrictive ("Clear," Rule 281, indicating "Proceed") to most restrictive ("Stop," Rule 292). Most railroad rulebooks adopted these numbers, and retained the essential phrasing of AAR rules with only minor differences. As previously mentioned, signal aspects vary between individual rulebooks.

"Limited Speed" was re-introduced after the 1912 upper-quadrant semaphore aspects, so new distinct "Limited Speed" aspects were devised that conformed within the existing structure. Many railroads used

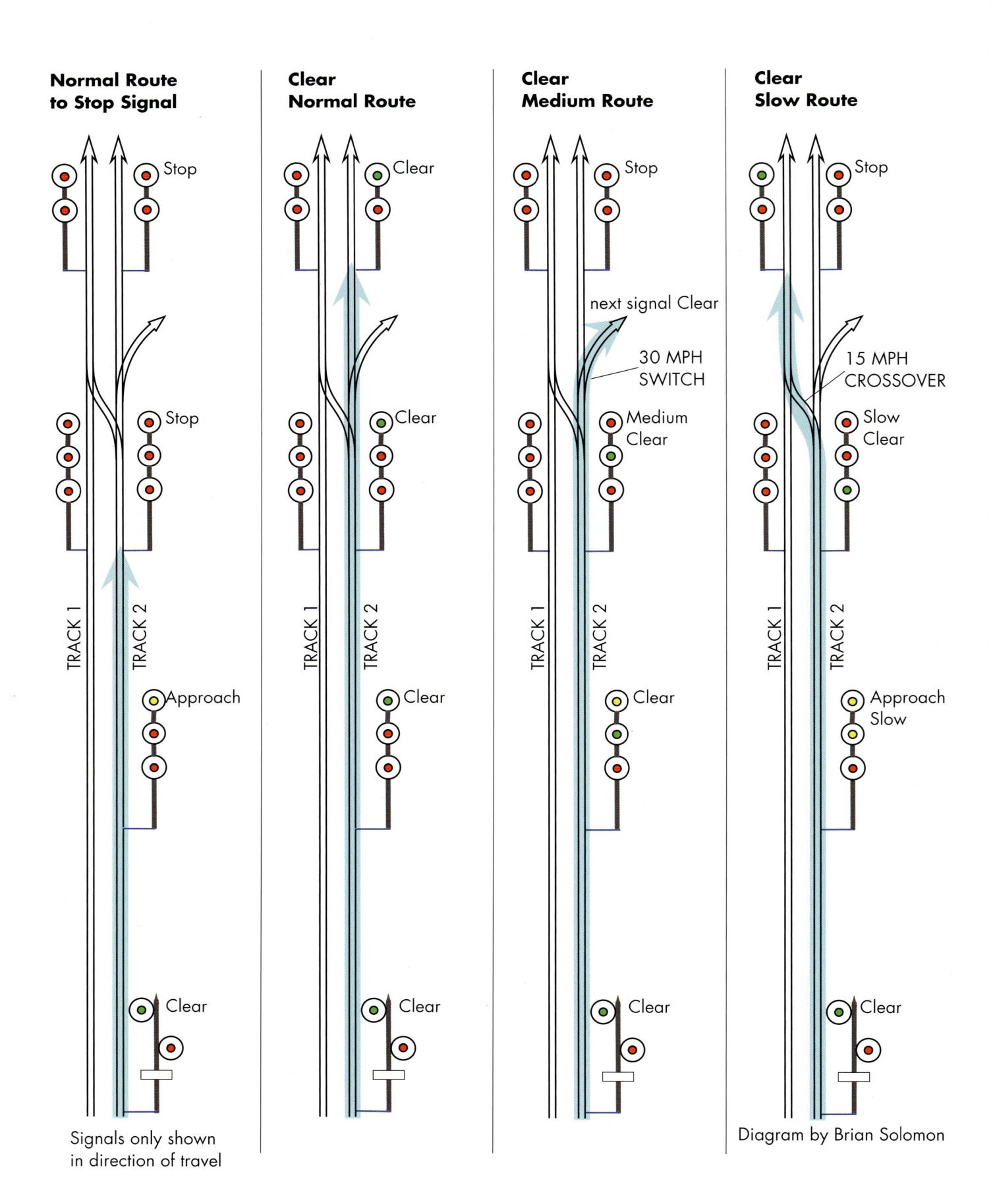

Normal Route to Stop Signal | Clear Normal Route | Clear Medium Route | Clear Slow Route

Normal Route to Stop Signal
- Stop / Stop
- Stop
- Approach
- Clear
- TRACK 1 / TRACK 2
- Signals only shown in direction of travel

Clear Normal Route
- Stop / Clear
- Clear
- Clear
- Clear

Clear Medium Route
- Stop
- next signal Clear
- 30 MPH SWITCH
- Medium Clear
- Clear
- Clear

Clear Slow Route
- Stop
- 15 MPH CROSSOVER
- Slow Clear
- Approach Slow
- Clear

Diagram by Brian Solomon

46   Chapter 2

Three-arm, upper-quadrant semaphores mounted on tall bracket post gantries were a common feature of interlocking signals on New York Central's Big Four route. These signals at Quincy, Ohio, survived into the Conrail era and were photographed with the setting sun on March 15, 1980. Notice that the blades in the third tiers (used to display slow-speed and restricting indications) use a slightly shorter blade. *John F. Bjorklund, courtesy of the Center for Railroad Photography & Art (www.railphoto-art.org).*

flashing light aspects for "Limited Speed" or modified "Medium Speed" aspects, using some fail-safe method to distinguish between the two speeds.

Pennsylvania Railroad identified "Limited Speed" position light signals by the addition of a yellow triangle. This effectively indicated to crews that "Medium Speed" aspects could be interpreted at the higher speed.

Advanced Warning

Trains approaching an interlocking signal displaying a cautionary aspect (one that restricts the speed of a train) require advanced warning. In most instances, one block advance warning is sufficient. These aspects provide necessary instructions for approaching the following signal(s) at a safe speed, while minimizing delays caused by approaching an interlocking with excessive caution.

In most instances, the order of the elements in the signal name provides vital information about the indication. When speed is mentioned first, this indicates the speed at which a train may pass that signal; when "Approach" appears first, it tells the crew at which speed they should approach the next signal. Thus "Medium Approach" is more restrictive than "Approach Medium."

1949 Interlocking Indications

Following the tradition in railroad rules since the nineteenth century, aspect names are capitalized.

Clear, Rule 281. Indicates "Proceed" and means the same as it does in automatic block territory. A variety of aspects may be used, especially where railroads have various arrangements of one-, two-, and three-head interlocking signals and/or dwarf signals.

Advance Approach Medium, Rule 281A. Indicates, "Proceed approaching second signal at

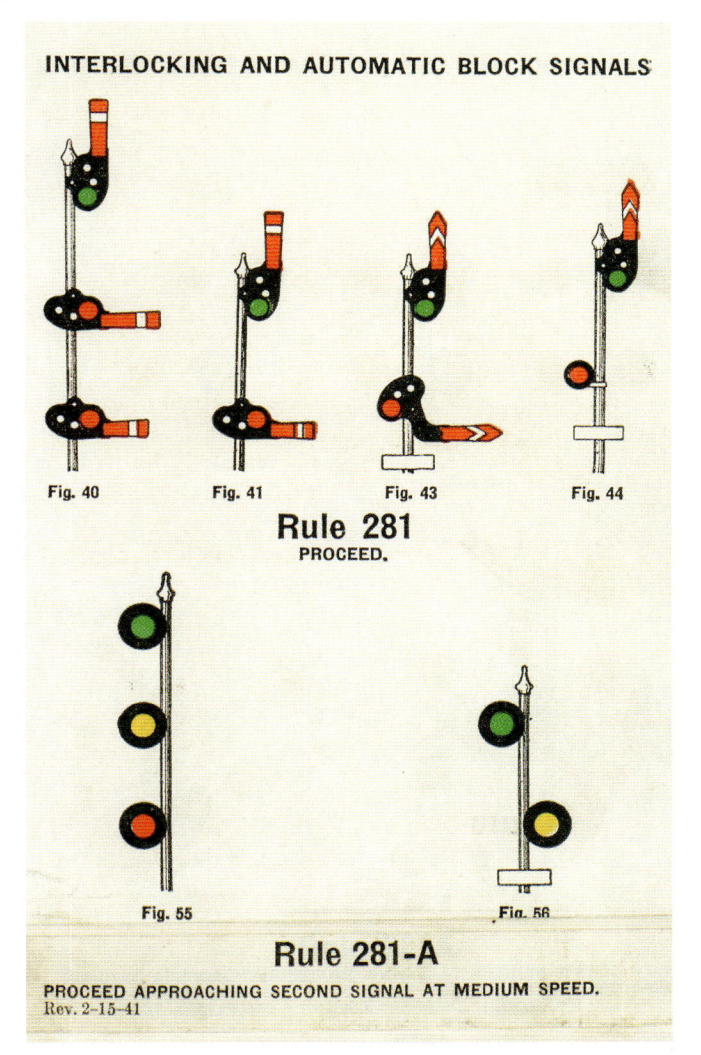

New York Central was only among a handful of railroads that used Rule 281A, known in the AAR 1947 signal code as "Advance Approach Medium," displayed by Central as a green-over-yellow. *Solomon collection*

Towers and Interlocking Signals **47**

281A

Fig. A   Fig B

INDICATION—Proceed approaching second signal at Medium Speed.
NAME   Advance Approach Medium.

281B

Fig A

INDICATION—Proceed approaching next signal at Limited Speed.
NAME   Approach Limited.

281C

Fig A

INDICATION—Proceed limited speed within Interlocking Limits.
NAME   Limited-Clear

282

Fig. A   Fig. B   Fig. C

INDICATION—Proceed approaching next signal at Medium Speed.
NAME   Approach Medium.

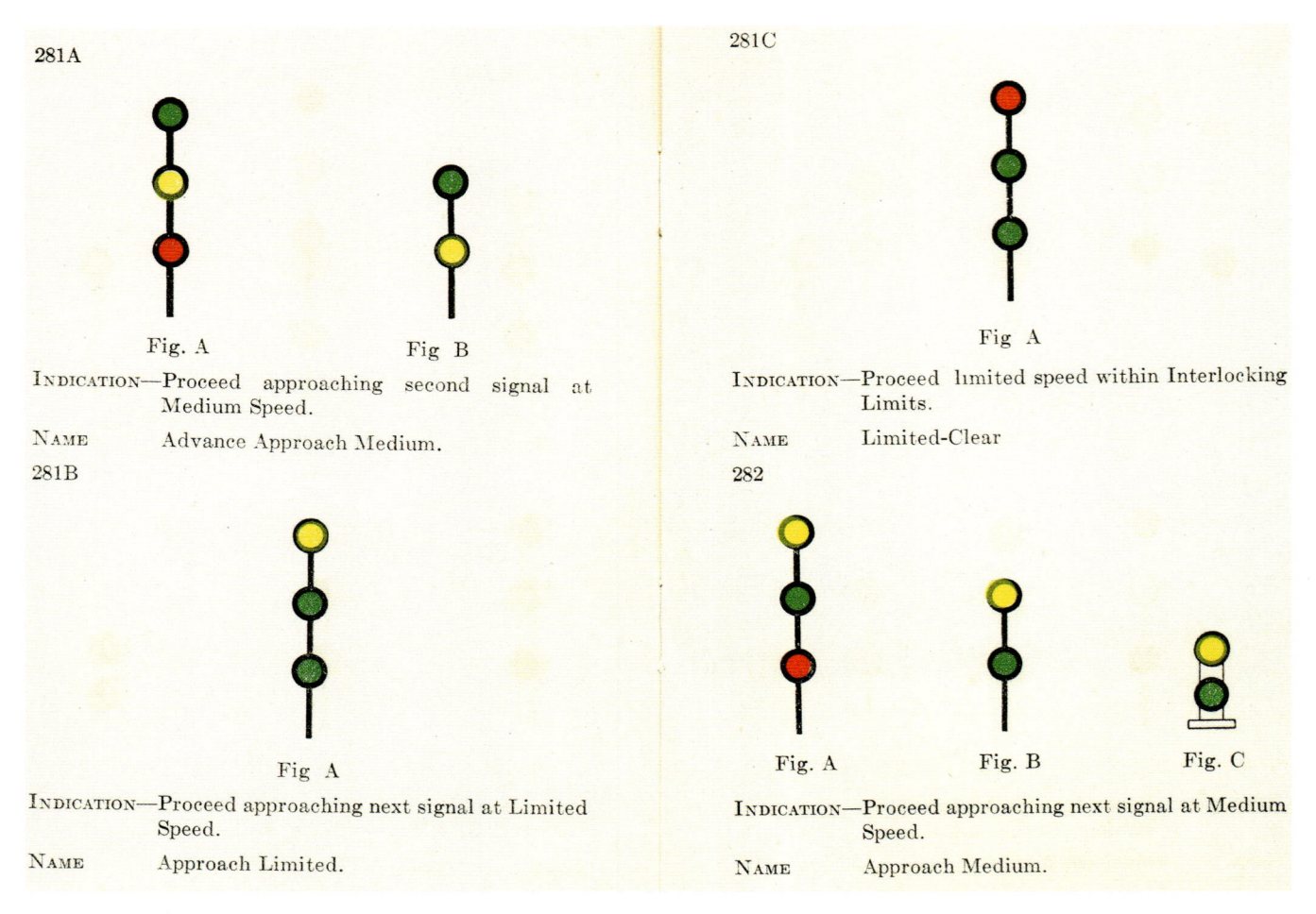

Western Maryland issued a rules supplement to its July 2, 1939, rulebook covering color light aspects and indications that went into effect on December 1, 1945. This included a variety of speed signal aspects not previously displayed by its semaphores. Among the more unusual aspects were those covered by Rules 281B "Approach Limited" and 281C "Limited Clear." Railroads using flashing aspects might display a single flashing green instead of two green lights. *Solomon collection*

medium speed," one of the more uncommon aspects defined by the 1949 code. New York Central was among the few railroads to have used it. This was applied in situations where four-aspect, three-block ABS is used in conjunction with a medium-speed interlocking route.

Approach Limited, Rule 281B indicates "Approach next signal at limited speed." In its classic interpretation, when 60 miles per hour was used for "Limited Speed," this indication advised the crew that they could proceed at normal speed, but approach the next signal at limited speed. This was used in advance of a "Limited Clear."

Limited Clear, Rule 281C indicates "Proceed, Limited Speed within interlocking limits." This tells the crew that they have a clear route through limited speed switches and then may resume normal speed once completely clear of the interlocking. As with a "Clear," it indicates that at least two full blocks ahead are clear. It would typically be preceded by an "Approach Limited."

Approach Medium, Rule 282 indicates "Proceed approaching next signal at Medium Speed." Similar to the case with an "Approach Limited," which informs the train crew to proceed while approaching the next signal at medium speed. It's one of the more common interlocking aspects because it can be used in advance of a signal displaying any of a variety of medium-speed aspects, including: "Medium Clear," "Approach," "Medium Approach," "Advance Approach," and even another "Approach Medium." Although rulebooks didn't specifically qualify the role of a signal's top arm/head, generally these were not used to authorize movements on diverging routes.

Although the descriptive name of this aspect sounds similar to "Medium Approach," the two aspects are

Signal Aspects Table 1

Searchlight*	Color Position Light	AAR Rule and Name
Green over red over red (various configurations)	White over green over green	Rule 281 Clear
Yellow over red; green over yellow	No Aspect	Rule 281A Advance Approach Medium
Yellow (F) over red; yellow over (F); yellow over (F) green	Flashing white over green over green	Rule 281B Approach Limited
Red over green (F); red over (F)	Green over green	Rule 281C Limited Clear
Yellow over green over red; yellow over green	White over green over green	Rule 282 Approach Medium
Yellow over green over red; yellow over yellow over green	No Aspect	Rule 282A Advance Approach
Red over green over red	Green over green over white	Rule 283 Medium Clear
Red over yellow over green	Green over green over yellow	Rule 283B Medium Approach Slow

Notes: Searchlight aspects based on New York Central 1937 rulebook; color position lights based on Baltimore & Ohio 1941 rulebook. Only high signal aspects shown; not all shown. Wording of indications may vary.

☀ ☼ = flashing light
▭ = number plate

Signal Aspects Table 2

Searchlight*	Color Position Light	AAR Rule and Name
Yellow over green	Yellow over green over yellow	Rule 284 Approach Slow
Yellow over red; yellow over red; yellow over red	White over yellow over yellow	Rule 285 Approach
Red over yellow	Yellow over yellow	Rule 286 Medium Approach
Red	Green over green	Rule 287 Slow Clear
Yellow (NYC Rule 289A*)	White over blue over blue (B&O)	B&O Rule 289A Medium Permissive
Red over yellow; yellow over red	Blue over blue over white	Rule 290 Restricting
Red over red	White over red over red	Rule 291 Stop and Proceed
Red over red; red over red	Red over red over red	Rule 292 Stop

Notes: Searchlight aspects based on New York Central 1937 rulebook; color position lights based on Baltimore & Ohio 1941 rulebook. Only high signal aspects shown; not all shown. Wording of indications may vary.

*NYC Rule 289A: block occupied; proceed prepared to stop short of train ahead. Slow speed must not be exceeded.

▭ = number plate

Towers and Interlocking Signals **49**

Canadian Pacific freight 413 received an "Approach Medium"—yellow over green over red—as it exited the siding at CPF 485 in Schenectady, New York, on April 16, 2005. CP's Delaware & Hudson routes had been largely equipped with General Railway Signal searchlights, but since 2005, most of this traditional hardware has been replaced with modern color lights. *Patrick Yough*

significantly different: an "Approach Medium" indicates there are at least two blocks clear ahead, while a "Medium Approach" suggests that only one block ahead is clear. The difference between these aspects is both the speed at which they may be passed and the distance a train may travel before it may be required to stop.

Medium Clear, Rule 283 indicates "Proceed, Medium Speed within interlocking limits." This tells the crew that they have a clear route through medium-speed switches and may resume normal speed once completely clear of the interlocking. "Medium Clear" is a common aspect and is often used for trains exiting sidings, or crossing from one main track to another, both situations where there are medium-speed switches involved.

Medium Approach Slow, Rule 283B indicates "Proceed at Medium Speed approaching next signal at Slow Speed." Another rarely used aspect, this indicates that there are medium-speed switches immediately beyond the signal while switches beyond the next signal are slow speed, yet the route remains clear for at least two signals. The next signal will display "Slow Clear."

Approach Slow, Rule 284 indicates "Proceed approaching next signal at Slow Speed. Train exceeding medium speed must at once reduce to that speed." This allows a train to proceed, with the caveat that it must prepare to pass through slow speed switches beyond the next signal, which may display "Slow Clear" or

50   Chapter 2

"Slow Approach," and thus indicates that the next two blocks are clear. Although similar in name to "Slow Approach," the two aspects should not be confused, as "Slow Approach" is more restrictive and indicates that train should be prepared to stop at the next signal (see below).

Approach, Rule 285 indicates "Proceed preparing to stop at next signal" sometimes with the further meaning "Train exceeding medium speed must at once reduce to that speed." This is a versatile aspect that has essentially the same meaning for an interlocking signal as it does for automatic block and may be followed by "Slow Clear," "Slow-Approach," "Restricting," "Stop and Proceed," or "Stop."

Medium Approach, Rule 286 indicates "Proceed at Medium Speed Preparing to Stop at Next Signal." This is very similar to a basic "Approach." It tells the crew that only one block ahead is clear and may be used at an interlocking where a train is using a medium-speed route and may be following another train, or approaching another interlocking. As with "Approach," the next signal may display; "Slow Clear," "Slow-Approach," "Permissive," "Restricting," "Stop and Proceed," or "Stop."

Slow Clear, Rule 287 indicates "Proceed at Slow Speed within interlocking limits." This is a common signal in terminals and is often displayed by dwarf signals. It indicates that the next two blocks are clear and that once a train has passed interlocking limits it may resume normal speed.

Slow Approach, Rule 288 indicates "Proceed prepared to stop at next signal; slow speed within interlocking limits." With some hardware styles, this aspect may only be displayed with a dwarf signal.

Restricting is among the most specialized signal aspects. It authorizes trains to "Proceed at Restricted Speed," which is not really a defined speed, but rather imposes a whole set of conditions (see Chapter 6). At interlockings "Restricting" is different than all other speed signals, because while it authorizes a train to proceed, it doesn't allow the resumption of normal speed once a train is beyond the interlocking, but rather instructs crews to expect an obstruction in the way. This aspect is often used to allow a train to enter an occupied track to couple to cars/engines positioned there, or to enter an un-signaled track (without track circuits) where conditions are unknown. In modern times, the Federal Railroad Administration (which assumed railroad safety oversight in the United States from the Interstate Commerce Commission) required very specific wording for "Restricting," and so railroads regulated by the FRA adopted identical wording.

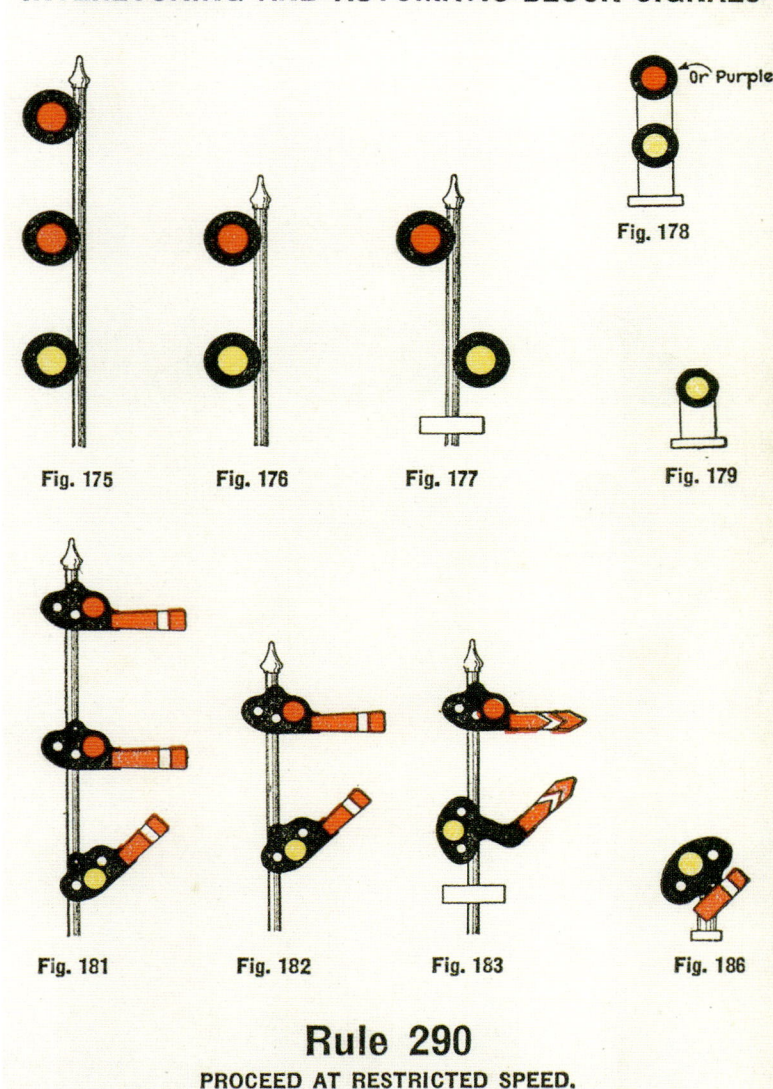

"Restricting" was among indications with the greatest variety of aspects. New York Central System's Rule Book (effective September 26, 1937) offered nine figures and ten different aspects showing rule 290, "Restricting"—note that figure 178 can display either a red or a purple light on top (thus counting as two aspects). *Solomon collection*

Towers and Interlocking Signals 51

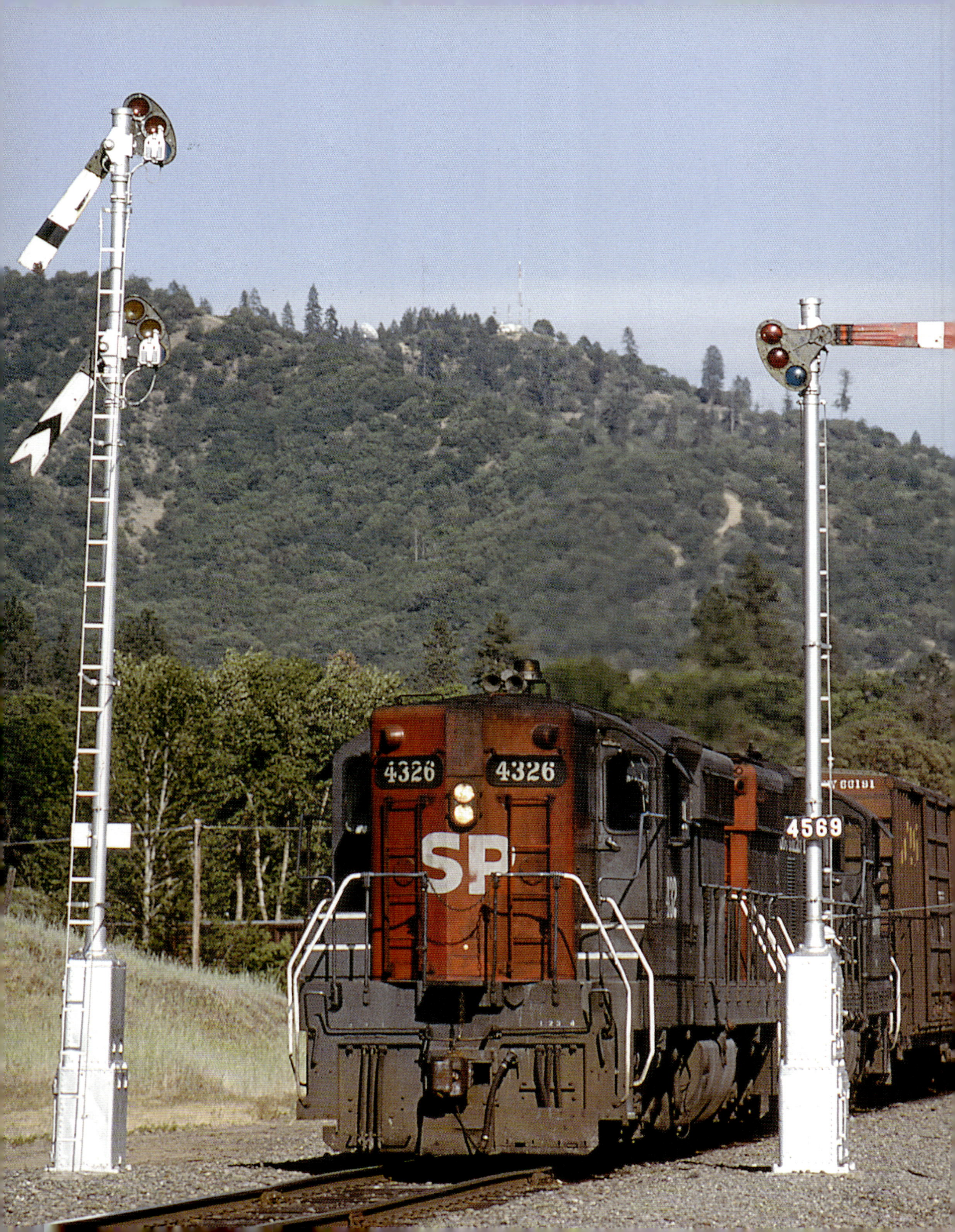
4326
4326
SP
4569

TWO-POSITION SEMAPHORES

3

Track Circuits

Railroad safety was a growing problem after the American Civil War, spurring inventor William Robinson to begin work on the electric track circuit in 1867. Robinson, heralded as the father of automatic block signaling, demonstrated his prototype track circuit in 1870. This relay-controlled circuit could detect a train on a section of track and actuate automatic signals. He filed for a United States patent for his closed track circuit on August 20, 1871, continued to refine the track circuit concept, and from 1873 was closely involved in pioneer automatic block signal systems. He eventually formed the Union Electric Signal Company in 1878. This became the core of Westinghouse's Union Switch & Signal Company (incorporated in 1881), which rapidly emerged as a leader in commercial American signaling systems and hardware.

Hall Disc Signals

The Hall Signal Company was another chief pioneer in commercial automatic block signaling. The company was founded in 1871 by inventor Thomas Seavey Hall of Hartford, Connecticut, whose work in devising an electrical signal mechanism paralleled Robinson's track circuit development.

In the early 1870s, Hall was among the first to offer a commercial block signal in the form of a disc signal—colloquially called the "banjo signal" because of its distinctive shape. Although the Hall disc was applied to a variety of applications, including interlocking signals, in the early days of automatic signaling it was one of the most common types of block signals.

The Hall disc-signal was a two-position signal made from a wood and metal frame that protected the disc and its mechanism from effects

53

of weather with a central circular display window, which either showed the disc or hid it from view, leaving the window open. In its more advanced design, the signal also displayed a lighted roundel for night indications. The premise of the two positions was that the signal was more restrictive when the disc was displayed.

In automatic block service, signals were typically arranged in pairs using the home and distant arrangement. The home signal would display "Stop/Danger" or "Proceed/Clear," while the distant signal would mimic the condition of the home signal and display "Stop and Proceed" and "Caution" aspects. Where home signals displayed a red disc for "Stop," the color used for cautionary distant signals varied from road to road; and depending on individual rulebooks displayed green, yellow, or even blue discs.

Hall Disc Mechanism

The Hall signal's success was a testimony to its simple fail-safe automatic operation at a time when commercial electrical appliances were in their infancy. The mechanical lower-quadrant semaphore was an accepted standard for interlockings, but during the 1870s–1880s the comparatively heavy semaphore blade required a more substantial and more complex electrical mechanism than could be manufactured cheaply or operated reliably. Also semaphores suffered in snow territory, where a semaphore blade might be pushed by a heavy load of snow, or where thawing snow might freeze in place thus gripping a semaphore blade and prevent it from moving to a more restrictive position.

By contrast, the disc in a Hall signal was lightweight, was easily moved by a relatively inexpensive and reliable electromagnetic mechanism, and was protected from the elements by a solid enclosure. The signal mechanism consisted of a simple Z-shaped armature as part of a dual electromagnet relay arrangement that operated a rod, which carried the cloth-covered disk (17 inches in diameter) and was balanced by a counterweight at the far end. Silk was typically used for a translucent disk covering. Signals that were designed to display a night aspect had a separate window for an oil lamp and the disc was balanced by a colored roundel (6.5 inches in diameter) to be displayed in front the lamp in the restrictive position.

When the track circuit showed clear, one relay rotated the rod to withdraw the disc/roundel from the window, while the second relay worked as a locking catch to hold the rod in place and thus keep the disc/roundel out of sight. In accordance with fail-safe operation, when

Disc Signal Instrument, Style A.

This detailed view of a Hall-style A disc signal instrument shows one type of relay-actuated mechanism used inside a disc signal. Hall's Reference Catalogue No. 4 offered four varieties of disc signal mechanisms, including a special variety for Chicago & North Western. The small discs were of colored glass while key moving components were made from aluminum. *Solomon collection*

the catch relay was de-energized it released the disc to return by gravity to display the disc. Any interruption of electric current, either from a train shunting a track circuit, or an electrical failure, automatically released the disc to display in the window.

Disc Signals on Illinois Central R. R., Chicago.

As of June 30, 1908, IC boasted 121 interlocking plants and more than 1,032 route miles protected by block signals. IC had several installations using Hall disc signals. The most intensive was 13.7 miles of multiple-track mainline south from Chicago's Van Buren Street to Kensington. Here Hall discs worked in conjunction with track circuit protection. *Hall Signal Company catalog, Solomon collection.*

Hall Disc Customers

Hall had devised its own systems for automatically actuating disc signals, but these involved awkward mechanical components that lacked both the simplicity and reliability of Robinson's track circuit. In later years, most successful commercial applications of Hall disc signals were in combination with track circuits.

Hall signals could be worked in either a normal-clear or normal-danger configuration. In the normal-danger arrangement, the signal displayed restrictive indications until cleared ahead of a train (provided the block was unoccupied). This added safety feature required additional control circuitry.

Photographs of Hall signals in service are relatively rare, but the signals were sold for four decades from the mid-1870s until the World War I era. Early customers included southern New England railroads: Boston & Lowell, Eastern Railroad, Boston & Albany, and New York, New Haven & Hartford. Boston & Albany was a Hall discs pioneer, with a documented installation by 1875. Delaware, Lackawanna & Western, Lehigh Valley, Michigan Central, Illinois Central, Chicago & North Western, and Oregon Short Line also had significant Hall disc installations. Chicago & North Western had its own variation of Hall signals that warranted a special mention in Hall's signal catalog.

There were a few competitors to the Hall disc, notably the Union Banner Signal sold by Westinghouse's Union Switch & Signal, which used similarly shaped signal housings.

Disc Signals on Lehigh Valley R. R.

While never as common as semaphores, disc signals were among the most common type of block signal in the early years of the twentieth century. In its 1901 catalogue, Hall boasted "We believe that . . . with the experience gained in the installation of more than 80 per cent of all the automatic, electric block signals on the railroads of the United States since 1890, we are justified in claiming to be more competent than any other company to furnish economical, efficient and reliable systems of automatic signals." The *Railway Gazette* reported that by 1904, there were 4,697 enclosed disc signals in automatic block service in the United States.

One of the largest, and certainly the most enduring Hall disc railroads was the Philadelphia & Reading, which continued to buy Hall discs until the eve of World War I; in 1914, it installed new Hall discs on several line sections, including: between Port Clinton and Tamaqua, Pennsylvania; between Tamaqua Tunnel and Mahonoy Tunnel; from Woodbourne to Yardley; and from Hopewell to Belle Meade. Notably, this occurred several years after the nearby Lackawanna had begun replacing Hall discs with lower-quadrant semaphores.

By 1916, Reading was installing new Federal Signal three-position semaphores on its line from Lewisburg to Newberry Junction, Pennsylvania. The railroad continued to maintain Hall discs in active block service until after World War II, decades longer than most other railroads with this early signal hardware. A handful of Hall discs survive in museums and private collections.

◐ Hall's Reference Catalogue No. 4 used this photo of a dual-head disc signal in automatic block service on Lehigh Valley in Pennsylvania's Lehigh River gorge. The number displayed on the top head was used to identify specific signals. *Hall Signal Company catalog, Solomon collection.*

◐ Reading Company class K1sb 2-10-2 3011 leads a westward freight at Emmaus, Pennsylvania. Hall disc signals in automatic block service are arranged as a home and distant on common mast. This provided effectively the same aspects as a twin-arm, lower-quadrant semaphore in block service. The signal at right is at its most restrictive, displaying a red disc on top and a yellow disc below. *Donald W. Furler*

◐ Reading was the last railroad to use Hall disc signals. In this unusual signal at East Rutherford, Pennsylvania, a mechanical, wire-operated, lower-quadrant semaphore shares a mast with a pair of Hall discs. Notice the semaphore counterweight below the semaphore arm. Eastward freight HJ-6 is led by Reading Company class T-1 4-8-4 2103. *Donald W. Furler*

56 Chapter 3

Two-Position Semaphores 57

Lower-Quadrant Semaphore Practice

The two-position, lower-quadrant semaphore had evolved in Britain as an early standard for railroad signaling. In America it was adopted for interlocking service and as a train order and manual block signal.

Since Union Switch & Signal's (US&S) parent was air brake pioneer Westinghouse, the company enthusiastically promoted air-powered devices, including signaling equipment. In 1882, Pennsylvania Railroad experimentally installed US&S electropneumatic lower-quadrant semaphores. Compressed air was supplied from a remote air compressor powered by a stationary steam engine. An electromagnet-actuated valve admitted air into a cylinder, which acted on rods to move the

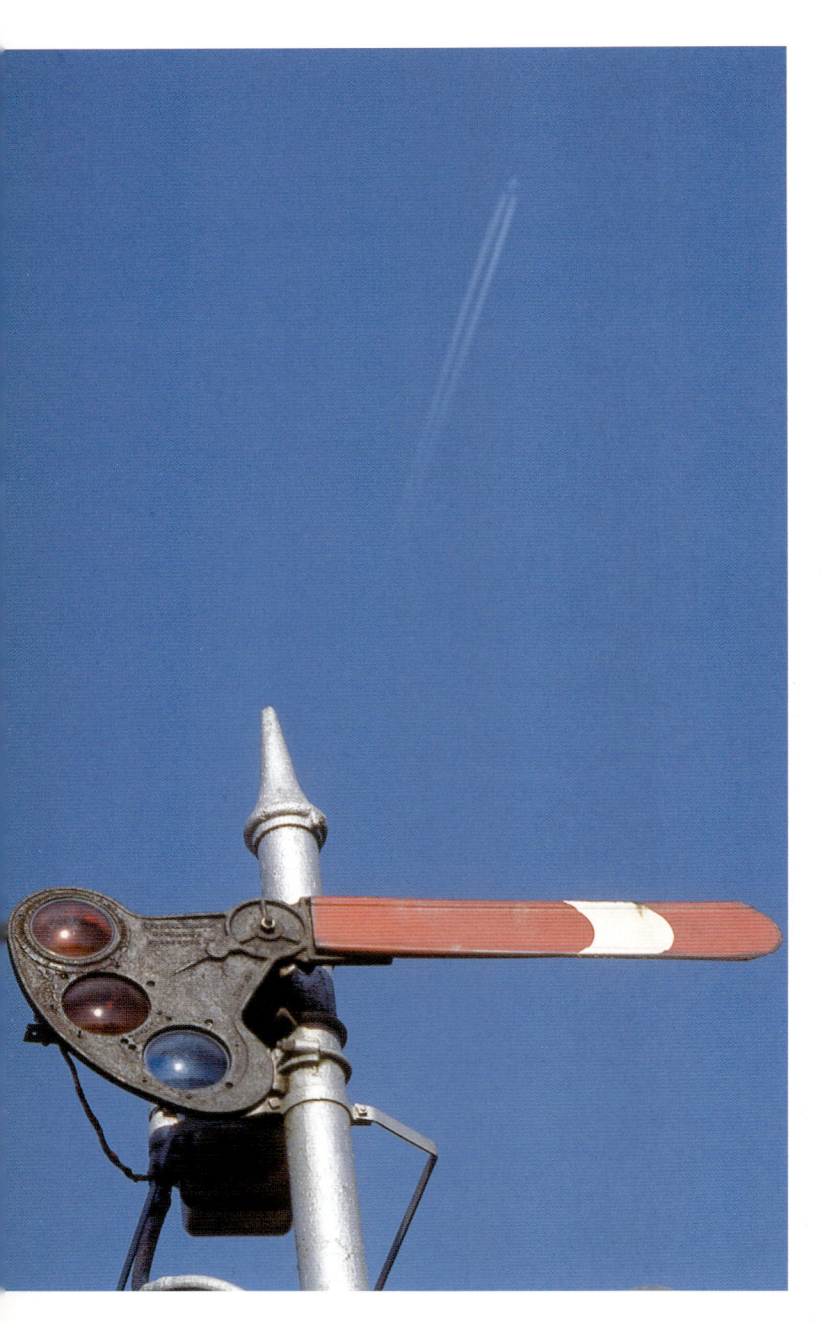

⊕ Contrasts in technology: an enameled lower-quadrant semaphore blade against the backdrop of a jet's contrail. This signal was located on the former New Haven Railroad at Walpole, Massachusetts. Historically, this had been the location of the first interlocked crossing in New England, installed by Britain's W. R. Sykes Interlocking Signal Company Ltd in 1881, although this signal dates from a later period, possibly from the time of a more modern interlocking built at South Walpole in 1913. *Brian Solomon*

⊕ On March 2, 1988, a Massachusetts Bay Transportation Authority suburban train works west on the Franklin Line at Walpole, Massachusetts. The old semaphores were in their final months. Today the crossing is protected by color lights. *Brian Solomon*

58   Chapter 3

On the Chicago L, one- and two-arm, lower-quadrant low signals were standard equipment. In later years electric color lights replaced most semaphores, but a few antiques survived into the 1990s, such as this signal to facilitate reverse moves. Chicago Transit Authority's interlocking rules used a lunar aspect to indicate "Proceed Expecting To Encounter End Of Track Or Train Ahead." *Brian Solomon*

semaphore arm into its less restrictive (45-degree lower diagonal) position. The blade was counterweighted to allow gravity to restore it to the horizontal position when air pressure was released from the cylinder. This mechanism was a relative success, which led to PRR's more extensive applications of pneumatic ABS signals.

Despite this early application, automatic lower quadrants remained relatively unusual in the nineteenth century. Advances in electric motor technology in the late 1890s finally made it possible to develop commercial two-position, all-electric semaphores for block service.

Following precedents established by British home and distant semaphore practices, home signals (indicating an absolute stop) used red flat-ended blades with a white stripe, while distant blades featured a fishtail shape (an inverted chevron) colored either green or yellow. A distant signal provided advance warning as to the condition of the home signal (by mimicking that signal), yet did not itself provide information as to the condition of the track between it and the home signal.

PRR was one of the earliest American lines to establish British semaphore practices for American automatic signals. Significantly, American semaphores were mirrors of their British counterparts, owning to the preference in the USA for the engineer run on the right versus the British preference to run on the left. American block semaphores tended to be oriented to the right of the track they governed, and semaphore blades pivoted to the right (moving away from the track as they turned toward the horizontal position).

In British mechanical signaling practice when the top blade was in the horizontal position and the lower arm displayed clear, it indicated a diverging proceed (often used to indicate entry into a siding). While most American automatic block systems didn't use this aspect, it was likely the origin of the various diverging clear aspect as applied to interlocking signals.

White stripes/chevrons near the ends of semaphore blades were designed to aid in sighting in low light and at night. Long burning oil lamps provided night aspects through roundels at the spectacle-end of the semaphore arm.

Motor Semaphores

A 1912 article by J. S. Hobson in *The Signal Engineer* chronicled pioneer moments in motor semaphore development. In 1897, electropneumatic interlocking genius John Pressley Coleman patented a successful electric motor lower-quadrant semaphore. This featured a mechanism in the signal base with connections enclosed in the mast to operate the semaphore arm. Among early applications of this design were signals at Detroit's Michigan Central Depot. A further advancement was credited to V. K. Spicer who used a slot arm powered by a motor-driven bicycle chain.

Once perfected, the motor-operated, lower-quadrant semaphore rapidly became the dominant hardware for automatic block service. On the eve of the twentieth century, there were only about 200 all-electric

Motor Mechanism, Double Signal, Style D.

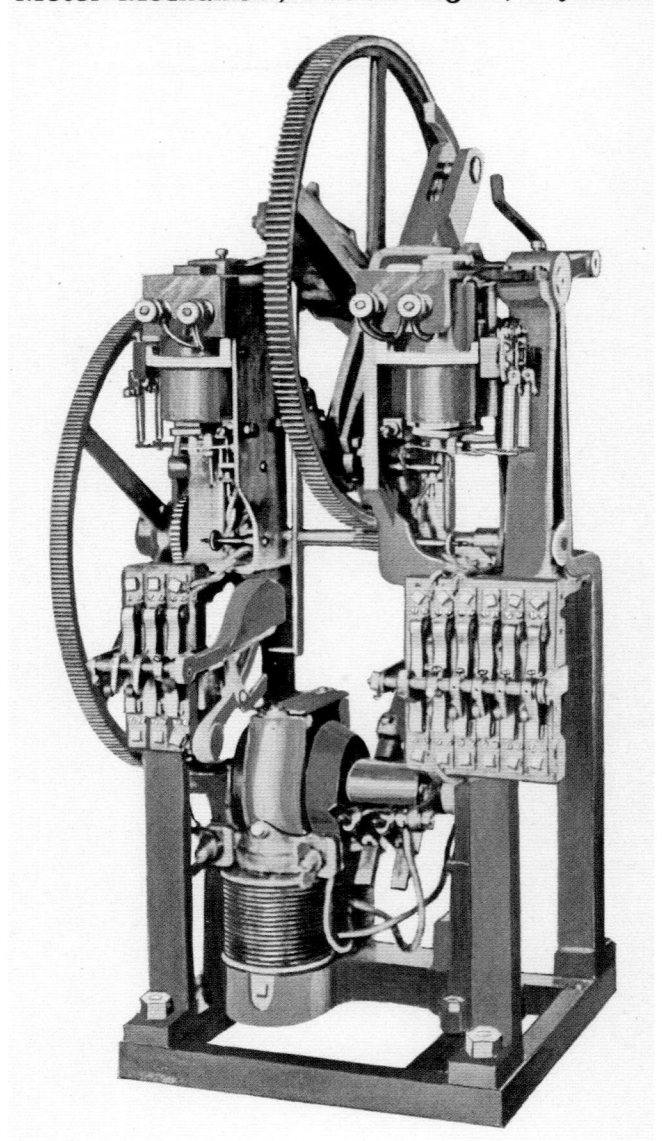

The Hall Signal Company's Reference Catalogue No. 4, published in 1901, listed three varieties of motor-semaphore mechanisms. This Style D is set up for a twin-arm, lower-quadrant signal. *Solomon collection*

60   Chapter 3

semaphores in the United States; within five years nearly 7,000 all-electric semaphores were protecting American lines. Although the all-electric semaphore was the preferred type of hardware, it didn't immediately supersede the electropneumatic type. Yet, by 1908, the lower-quadrant, all-electric semaphore had reached the zenith of its popularity.

Hall and US&S were both motor-operated, lower-quadrant pioneers. Although Hall continued to promote and sell its well-established disc signal, its 1901 catalogue listed three varieties of chain-driven, base-of-mast semaphore motor mechanisms: Styles C, D, and W.

More successful, and by far the most common lower-quadrant motor signal, was Union Switch & Signal's Style B base-of-mast mechanism. This was developed in 1898 blending technology devised by J. P. Coleman and V. K. Spicer and rapidly emerged as a standard type of hardware applied to two-position automatic signals.

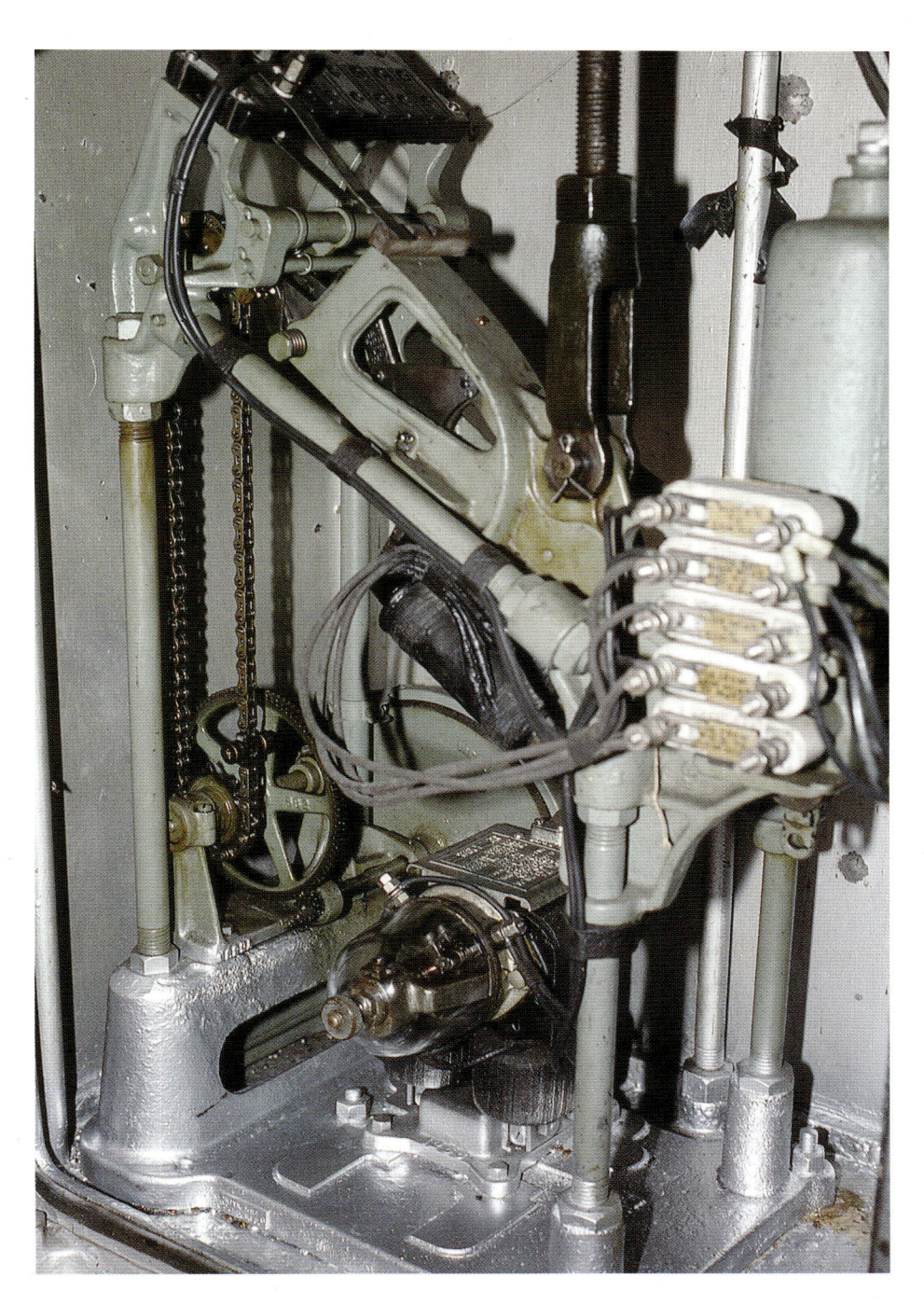

The Union Switch & Signal Style B semaphore mechanism was located at the base of the signal. This used an electric motor-powered, continuous-chain drive to move the rod that moved the blade into the clear position. The rugged quality of US&S signal machinery allowed these signals to serve continuously for decades. *Hal Reiser*

A two-position, lower-quadrant semaphore displays an "Approach" aspect, indicating "proceed, prepared to stop at next signal." *Brian Solomon*

The Style B motor shaft worked a pinion-driven continuous gear train. One of the chain links was a trunnion (a pivoting protrusion) designed to lift a slot arm connected with an up-down rod at the center of the signal mast that moved the signal arm from the horizontal to diagonal position. Once the signal arm was fully in the clear position, an electromagnet engaged the interior slot arm and held the signal rigid while hooks were caught by a pawl to lock it in place. Since the slot magnet must remain energized to keep the arm in the clear position, when it was de-energized the semaphore naturally returned to the horizontal position by gravity aided by counter weights. A dashpot cushioned the semaphore arm's descent to prevent it from damage. On twin-arm signals, one mechanism powered both home and distant arms using two chains, one for each.

Although most often used as an automatic block signal, the Style B could be fitted with manual controls for service as a manual block or train order semaphore. Since the signal would be controlled by an operator, the rules governing it would be different than those working in ABS service. Other commercial varieties of lower-quadrant motor semaphores included General Railway Signal (GRS) Model 3, 6, and 7 signals, and the Federal Signal Type 4.

During the first decade of the twentieth century, New York Ontario & Western made a large investment in Union Switch & Signal Style B lower-quadrant semaphores. When the railroad adopted the red-yellow-green color aspect progression in 1913, it equipped 145 route miles with ABS signaling. This US&S lower-quadrant semaphore was photographed in 1947 looking east at Merrickville, New York. NYO&W ended operations in 1957, and most of its lines were abandoned. *John E. Pickett*

Two-Position Semaphores 63

Style Bs on Boston & Maine

Boston & Maine (B&M) was an avid Style B road. In 1912 *The Signal Engineer* reported that B&M had protected 943 miles of track with an estimated 2,000 US&S Style B signals. In most respects these were typical for the period, working in the lower-right quadrant, with twin blades on each mast, the bottom using a fishtail blade that repeated the condition of the next signal. B&M had begun installing US&S Style Bs around 1906.

One unusual feature of B&M semaphore practice was a carryover from its use of banner signals: signals were wired so that as a train passed it the engineer would begin to see it drop. This was covered in the rulebook as follows:

> Rule 501A. The semaphore arm should start to change from [Proceed] to [Stop] as a train approaches within about one hundred feet of the signal. If a semaphore arm at proceed does not start to change on passing it, it should be regarded as if at [Stop], and the train brought to stop as soon as possible."

This non-standard system had two advantages: It encouraged the engineer to study the signal as he passed it and it ensured the signal was working properly and not frozen in the clear position. However, the obvious objection to this system was that it in effect required a train to routinely pass signals displaying "Stop."

Union Switch & Signal builders plate on the base of a Style B signal on the former Southern Pacific Siskiyou Line at Dole, Oregon, on April 23, 2003. Historically, SP embraced US&S hardware for most of its line-side signaling. *Hal Reiser*

Among the lines protected were: Portland Division (Boston to Portland via both Eastern and Western routes); Boston to White River Junction; Fitchburg Division (Boston to Rotterdam Junction, New York, except for 8 miles in the electrified zone through the 4.75-mile Hoosac Tunnel); South Ashburnham, Massachusetts to Bellows Falls, Vermont; Worcester to Ayer, Massachusetts; Concord to Woodsville, New Hampshire; Concord to Tilton, New Hampshire; and Johnsonville to Troy, New York.

Maine Central, which was closely affiliated with B&M in the early twentieth century, also adopted the twin-arm Style B lower-quadrant semaphore and by 1913 had 510 miles equipped with ABS signaling. Its signals were typically operated by caustic soda batteries, a common way of powering semaphores of the period.

Southern Pacific's Long-Lived Lower Quadrants

In the early twentieth century, Southern Pacific (SP), along with Union Pacific (UP) and its affiliated railroads, was controlled by E. H. Harriman. The Harriman administration was famous for implementing standardized equipment (bridges, locomotives, rolling stock), and for strict attention to safety. (To this day, annual Harriman Awards are given to railroads for excellent safety records.) Under Harriman, the US&S Style B lower-quadrant semaphore was introduced as the standard block signal on SP, UP, and affiliated railroads. Significantly, Southern Pacific embraced this semaphore for automatic block signaling to a greater extent than any other American railroad; SP clung to the Style B for new installations for more than a decade after more advanced signals had rendered it obsolete, and continued to maintain these signals on some lines into the 1990s.

Railway Signal Engineer credited SP's early ABS installations to the wisdom of the company's veteran signal engineer, W.W. Slater (who served for 30 years before retiring around 1913). SP began installing electropneumatic interlockings in Oakland about 1884, but didn't begin working with ABS signaling until 1901 when it signaled 30 miles of its heavily traveled route through California's Tehachapi Mountains.

By 1908, SP already boasted the most extensive application of electric semaphore ABS. On its Pacific Lines it had 1,752 miles of track protected by US&S Style B signals. Slater's signaling standards prevailed over Harriman's other roads—Union Pacific signaled 1178 miles, while UP's Oregon Short Line and Oregon Railway & Navigation subsidiaries combined had more than 450 miles protected.

◉ Southern Pacific SD9s work the Grants Pass Turn as it passes by World War I–vintage Union Switch & Signal Style B lower-quadrant semaphores at Gold Hill, Oregon, on the Siskiyou Line in April 1990. *Brian Solomon*

◉ In steam days, an engineer's sightline was limited by the narrow right-hand side view down the length of the boiler that dictated signal placement. This view of Southern Pacific's two-arm lower quadrants situated back-to-back at Kane, Oregon, was a rare exception in semaphore practice. The "fireman's side" semaphore was necessitated by tight clearance on the far side of the line. *J.D. Schmid*

SP's Siskiyou Line in far northern California and southern Oregon was among several SP routes that retained large concentrations of Style Bs into the 1990s. The Siskiyou had been built as part of SP's primary route to Oregon in the 1880s, largely equipped with Style Bs during World War I. It was bypassed in the late 1920s with completion of a highly engineered route via Cascade Summit, but survived as a through secondary line. As a result, after the early 1920s, SP made few infrastructure improvements to the Siskiyou Line and so the antique signaling was adequate decades after more advanced protection was implemented elsewhere on the SP system. In 1994, SP transferred operation of the Siskiyou Line to RailTex's Central Oregon & Pacific, and some Style B semaphores survived there for another decade.

Two-Position Semaphores   65

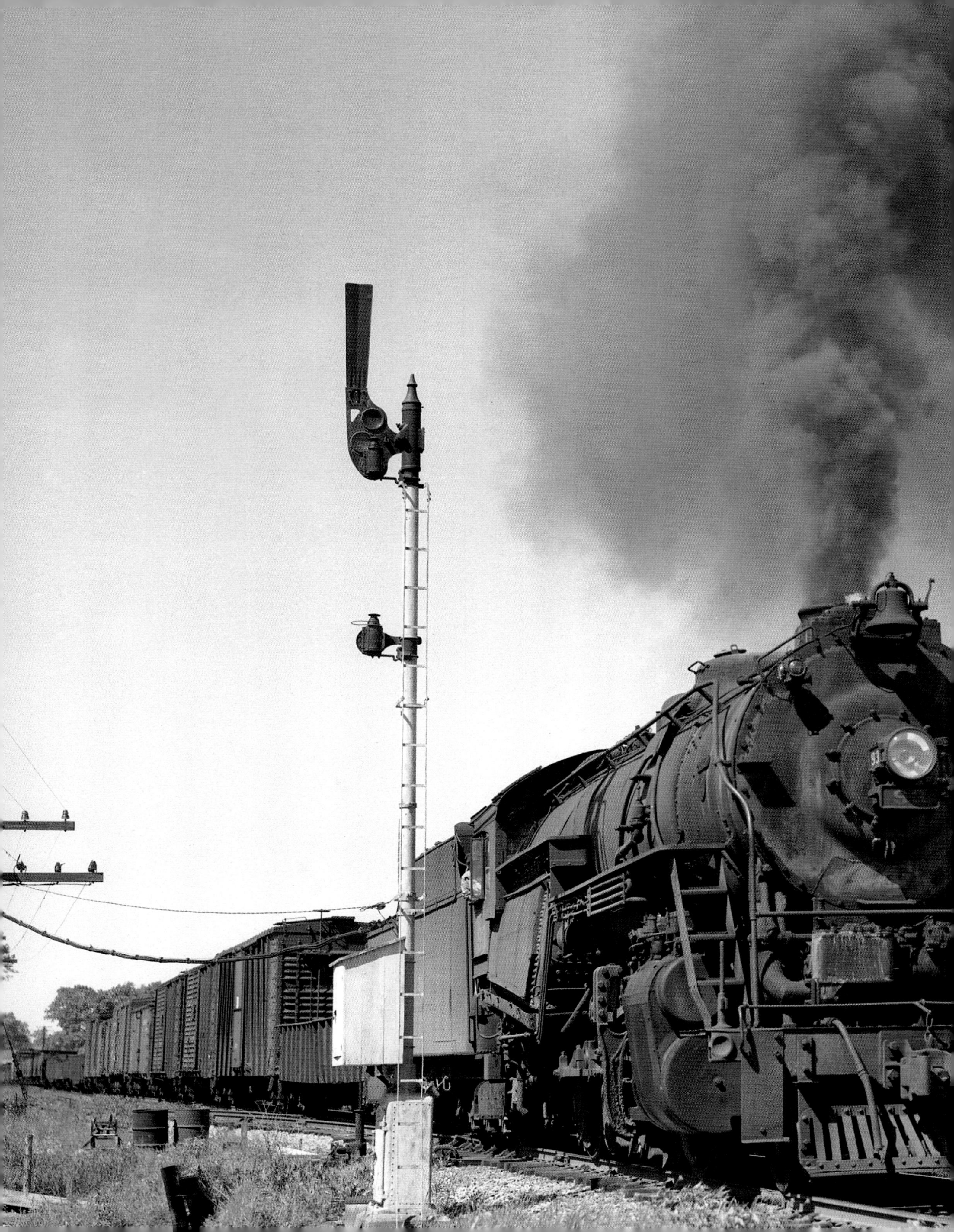

UPPER-QUADRANT SEMAPHORES

4

The New Standard Signal

By the early twentieth century, the traditional two-position, lower-quadrant semaphore was by far the most recognizable signal used in North America. Yet, because it displayed only two aspects, it was limited as both an interlocking and an automatic block signal. By contrast, a single-blade, three-aspect automatic block signal combined home and distant signals, and thus simplified the visual instruction given to the locomotive engineer and reduced the amount of equipment trackside. This also lowered costs and reduced the chance of equipment failure.

Three-aspect semaphores gained additional advantages as interlocking signals by allowing greater numbers of aspects with just two or three arms. With revised rules, three-aspect semaphores made it possible to reduce the maximum number of signal arms on individual interlocking signals from five to three.

Pioneer Three-Position Application

The three-position, upper-quadrant signal was not a new idea. In 1887, J. C. Cox and W. P. Black of Louisville, Kentucky, were issued United States patent 356,573 for a mechanical three-position, upper-quadrant semaphore, which described the signal as: "an improvement in semaphores adapted for use with a single or double track main track system, and has for its object to enable the operator to communicate accurately with trains at a distance the condition of the block or track while trains are under full speed or otherwise."

The invention combined semaphore blades and colored lenses to give both day and night aspects. This arrangement used the old R-G-W standard progression of colors. Their patent specified that a danger signal be displayed when the arm was at a horizontal with a red light at

67

night. The signal displayed its cautionary aspect with the arm at the midway diagonal with a green light at night while a vertical position, "indicates a safety-signal by day and the unobstructed white light [as] a safety signal by night."

This established the basic pattern for the type of signal later adapted for three-position automatic block service. In August 1909, *The Signal Engineer* reported that the first known application of the Cox and Black three-position semaphore was by the Kentucky & Indiana Bridge Company on the Kentucky & Louisville Belt Line & New Albany Belt & Terminal Railway in 1887, which operated 10.5 miles of line accommodating up to 425 movements daily.

Electropneumatic and Electrogas Semaphores

In lieu of practical electric motors, signal manufacturers devised alternative means of remotely operating semaphore arms. Electropneumatic (air) and electrogas (carbonic acid gas) two- and three-position semaphores were adapted and applied for automatic block service. These used electric actuation of compressed air or gas to move the semaphore arm into its less restrictive aspects (still described as "safety" for vertical and "caution" for diagonal), while relying on gravity to restore the signal to its most restrictive aspect ("danger"—horizontal).

American Railway Signaling Principles and Practices described the electrogas mechanism:

> The electrogas signal is operated by means of carbonic acid gas stored under pressure and was used to quite some extent before the electric semaphore signal was developed.
>
> Gas was admitted to a cylinder which operated the signal arm by means of a valve controlled by an electromagnet similar to that used in the electropneumatic signal. Gas was provided in tanks at a pressure of 600 to 1200 pounds per square inch and reduced for use to between 40 and 60 pounds by a pressure-reducing valve.

Union Switch & Signal was early to develop three-position semaphores, and in 1907 made a significant installation of electropneumatic semaphores along PRR's Middle Division (which extended across central Pennsylvania, west of Harrisburg to Altoona).

The shift from R-G-W to R-Y-G as standard color aspects generally coincided with the acceptance of three-position semaphores as standard for signal aspects, yet there were many holdouts. Before World War I, several large railroads, including PRR, adhered to the old standard, and installed three-position signals with the R-G-W arrangement.

On September 14, 1978, a US&S Style S upper-quadrant semaphore displays "Approach" with its blade at a 45-degree angle and a yellow light illuminated. Located in automatic block service on Santa Fe at Christie siding in California's Franklin Canyon, this was among signals that served for six decades. *J.D. Schmid*

On its Coast Lines, Santa Fe preferred US&S Style S (base-of-mast mechanism). In 1917, it installed ABS with Style S signals on approximately 200 miles from Fresno to Ferry Point, California. Venerable Style S signals display "clear" at Gately, California, on August 24, 1978. *J.D. Schmid*

On September 19, 1980, a view east on the Santa Fe at the end of the siding at Port Chicago, California, finds a Style S displaying "Approach," reflecting the position of westward train 199 that would soon pass. Semaphores in basic ABS service reflect conditions of track circuits: A train entering a block would shunt the circuit, causing signals protecting the block to display "Stop" or "Stop and Proceed," while those in the adjacent blocks would display "Approach." *J.D. Schmid*

Upper-Quadrant Semaphores

Upper-quadrant Patents
The basic pattern for an upper-quadrant semaphore as commonly used in North American dates back to 1903. The patent was awarded in July, 1903, to Leonor F. Loree (1858–1940) and Frank P. J. Patenall. Both men earned their place in American railroad history.

Loree was an energetic man with a long railroad résumé. He is probably best remembered for his long reign as president (1907–1938) of Delaware & Hudson (D&H) during which he unsuccessfully tried to implement a bold vision for a fifth-trunk line, and pushed D&H's experimental advancement of high pressure compound steam locomotive design.

Loree's early career was closely tied to the Pennsylvania Railroad, arguably the most influential railroad in the United States and one of the great shapers of North American signal practice. Loree was a product of a broad Victorian education having studied history and philosophy, while earning a bachelor of science in engineering from Rutgers University.

In the 1880s, he served in various engineering capacities for PRR, eventually earning the position of general manager of its Lines West (routes west of Pittsburgh). In 1901, he became a PRR Vice President, and PRR's visionary leader Alexander Cassatt installed him as president of Baltimore & Ohio. This was in the era before strict government regulation and anti-trust legislation, when PRR sought to closely control lines in its sphere of influence.

Loree's individualist approach benefited B&O and other railroads during his brief reign that lasted less than three years. During this time he not only influenced B&O signaling practice, but made other industry-changing decisions, such as encouraging the

World War II–era Baldwin 2-8-8-4 EM-1 7618 leads Baltimore & Ohio train 97 westward with 103 cars below the four-track signal bridge at Orleans Road, West Virginia (where the east end of B&O's Magnolia Cutoff short-cut rejoined B&O's older sinuous mainline). The semaphores pictured here are interlocking home signals controlled by the Orleans Road tower. The second set of signals displays a "Medium Clear" aspect (middle blade raised). *Donald W. Furler*

railroad's adaptation of the Mallet compound as a heavy road locomotive.

Frank P. J. Patenall was among the great voices in American signaling during the early twentieth century. Born in Britain, he began his signaling career in Manchester on the Lancashire & Yorkshire Railway. He was later employed by Union Switch & Signal constructing signal systems on English railways. In 1888, he emigrated to America to become signal engineer for Baltimore & Ohio, a position he held for four decades. Patenall served actively with the Railway Signaling Association and was an early proponent of three-position semaphore signaling as well as being a vocal advocate for the R-Y-G color progression. He is best remembered for development of B&O's color position light system featured in Chapter 6.

Loree's and Patenall's patent, No. 733,981, specified that the semaphore was mounted at the top of the mast and would pivot around the spectacle casting frame consisting of "two or more—preferably three—openings . . . arranged in circular series around a center . . . forming the pivotal axis on which the spectacle-casting turns. The spectacle-casting, it will be noted, is located practically all at one side of its pivotal center . . . Thus under the influence of gravity it will hang beneath the said center . . . In this preferred construction the weight of the parts is preferable so proportioned that if left entirely free, as would be the case should any of the operating connections become broken or disarranged, the spectacle-casting and blade or arm will of themselves assume the horizontal position or position of danger, thus blocking the track until the apparatus is again put in order."

Late in the steam-era, B&O Pacific number 5000 leads a westward express at Orleans Road. At the time of these photos, B&O was making a transition from World War I–era upper-quadrant semaphores to its distinctive color position light (CPL) hardware. In 1913, B&O began installing upper-quadrant automatic block semaphores on the Magnolia cutoff, then in 1916 it was reported to have installed General Railway Signal Model 2A upper quadrants for automatic block protection on its mainline between West Cumbo, Orleans Road, Magnolia, and Cumberland, Maryland. *Donald W. Furler*

The patent further specified preferred operation using a crank-arm attached to the spectacle-cast using "a counterweighted double bell-crank lever" located at the bottom of the mast and "push or pull rods extending to the tower, switch, or other control point being connected with the bell crank lever."

Significantly this stated, "in operation it is designed that the blade or arm shall be extended horizontally for 'danger,' or upwardly inclined to indicate 'caution,' or vertically upward to indicate 'safety' or 'clear track,' and it will be noted that because of the location of the spectacle-casting and arm or blade all at one side of the pivotal axis of the semaphore not only is the normal tendency to return to the danger position, but accumulations of snow or ice on the blade and casting increase this tendency, and consequentially should such accumulations be sufficient to break or distort the operating mechanism the result will be to set the semaphore to 'danger' or 'caution,' thereby preventing collision or accidents from this cause."

The patent specified that the three spectacle openings were for use of "transparent discs" used in conjunction with "a light or lantern" for colored night aspects. As might be expected for 1903, the colors specified were red for danger, green for caution, and white for safety.

A provision allowed for the signal arm to be used below the horizontal position, and thus allowed for five distinct positions, giving the semaphore up to five aspects.

Loree and Patenall assigned their patent to The Hall Signal Company that designed and manufactured commercial upper-quadrant signal equipment. Clarence W. Coleman of Westfield, New Jersey was among the inventors focused on upper-quadrant signaling. His three-position motor signal Patent 907,106 filed September 27, 1907, described his innovation as: "a mechanism to effect the cautionary and clear indication of a three-position semaphore by one semaphore actuating mechanism, in which the semaphore moving rod is given certain limited lengths of movement corresponding to the positions of the semaphore blade."

In addition, Coleman patented various three-position semaphore arrangements that offered advancements on earlier designs. In Patent 882,929, granted March 24, 1908, Coleman stated,

> "My invention relates to semaphores such as disclosed in the Loree and Patenall Patent . . . wherein the semaphore-blade moves through the upper-quadrant and the weight of snow and ice upon the semaphore-blade, instead of being an element of danger, is an element of safety, increasing the normal tendency of the semaphore to the danger position . . . its principal object to provide a semaphore having one or more spectacle-openings on one side of its pivot and weighted on the other side of its pivot independently of the blade so as to go to danger by gravity whether assisted by the blade or further assisted by snow and ice on the blade . . . so that the spectacle portion would go to danger at all times and under all conditions except when forcibly moved to clear by the operating mechanism."

Hall blended some of Coleman's innovations with the Loree and Patenall concept and other technology to produce a commercially successful three-position, motor-operated, upper-quadrant semaphore at precisely the time when three-position signaling was gaining acceptance as a preferred style of hardware.

A full-page advertisement by Hall in the October 1909 *The Signal Engineer* reveals an episode in the upper-quadrant story:

> The Loree-Patenall upper-quadrant semaphore, the joint invention of a distinguished railroad executive and an eminent signal engineer, is the semaphore *par excellence* of the signaling art. A series of most exacting scientific tests has proved its superiority over every other form of semaphore. No better proof of the accuracy of this statement can be furnished than the following list of companies licensed to manufacture and sell this signal:
> "General Electric Company
> "Westinghouse Electric and
>   Manufacturing Company
> "American Railway Signal Company, and
> "Federal Signal Company
> The Hall Signal Company will hereafter exercise its discretion as to granting or refusing licenses under its semaphore patents and all public offers of license are hereby withdrawn. Against all infringers The Hall Signal Company will enforce its legal rights under its patents, which include Loree & Patenall Patent No. 733,981, and C.W. Coleman patents Nos. 882,928, 882,929, 882,930, all for upper-quadrant semaphores.

In the same advertisement, Hall announced it was pursuing a suit for infringement of the Loree & Patenall patent by the General Railway Signal Company.

Despite legal wrangling, GRS continued to develop and market upper-quadrant signaling, having introduced its Model 2A mechanism in 1908. Various suits between the primary manufactures of signal equipment continued to hamper development and application of signaling systems until 1916 when the four primary signal manufacturers, Federal Railway Signal, General Railway Signal, Hall Switch & Signal (having changed its name following reorganization in 1912), and Union Switch & Signal entered a mutually-beneficial cross licensing agreement covering a variety of patents. This was designed to effectively end litigation between them, while allowing companies to blend various inventions to allow for safer signaling systems. At the time, *Railway Signal Engineer* proclaimed the settlement as one of the most important developments in American signaling.

Upper-Quadrant Motor Signals

The upper-quadrant electric semaphore was widely adopted for automatic block service after 1908. In 1912, the Railway Signal Association officially recommended the three-position, upper-quadrant semaphore for continuous ABS service in place of two-position signals using the home and distant system.

This signal became popular with North American railroads at a time when many lines were introducing or expanding existing automatic block. Its popularity coincided with key changes to signaling practice and new standard aspects.

Hall Upper Quadrants

By the early twentieth century, the Hall Signal Company was well established as a manufacturer of automatic block signaling and its early adoption of the three-position semaphore made it a logical supplier of this hardware.

Hall offered several types of upper-quadrant electric semaphores, and gradually improved its designs. A Hall advertisement in *The Railway Gazette* in December 1909 proclaimed the advantages of its Style H "top of mast" signal. This "simple compact design" enabled application of the mechanism with existing posts (mast) and spectacle castings. Powered by an 8-volt battery, it could be arranged to move the blade through a 60-degree arc in just five to six seconds. A clutch was used to hold the semaphore in the clear position. Interestingly, the advertisement showed a photo of a three-position, lower-quadrant signal, and indicated that the mechanism could be used in any combination of two or three positions in upper or lower quadrants.

By 1912, Hall had perfected its improved Style K semaphore. This top-of-mast signal was advertised in *The Signal Engineer* in January 1912. Hall explained that it endeavored "to design signals that will operate safely and reliably under most unfavorable conditions and with improper maintenance." Among its features was rugged all-weather design using floated ball bearings and bronze gears (intended to avoid corrosion). This could be adapted for either upper- or lower-quadrant applications, with direct current or alternating current variations.

In 1916, Hall introduced its Style L semaphore mechanism that was significantly different than its older types. It was powered by a bi-polar motor to move the signal arm through a geared mesh and used electrical means to retard the arm on its return to the horizontal position. The signal was designed for both ABS and interlocking service and a variation of the mechanism was available for AC power. Although designed as a side clamp mechanism for top-of-mast applications, it could also be modified for base-of-mast service.

New York Central's Hall Signals

In 1908, New York Central & Hudson River Railroad began replacing controlled manual block signaling with Hall upper-quadrant electric semaphores on its Water Level route. The *Railway Signal Engineer* reported that the railroad had 124.7 route miles consisting of 278.4 track miles protected by electric semaphores by early 1909. Among the installations in place were the Hudson Division between Croton and Rhinecliff, from Yosts to Utica on the Mohawk Division, and west toward Buffalo between Batavia to East Buffalo. In 1912, Central installed Hall Style K upper quadrants between Greenway and Syracuse, and between Lyons and Rochester. It anticipated completing signaling with ABS on its passenger tracks of the Water Level Route by the end of 1913, and also was actively signaling connecting portions of its West Shore route, much of which was parallel with the multiple track Water Level main line.

New York Central's semaphores were normally positioned on through signal bridges with the signal masts supported by the lower deck of the bridge. Bridges were spaced roughly every five miles. Spacing of automatic signals was designed to reduce the number of interlockings and manned towers. Interestingly, when New York Central replaced Hall signals with searchlights between the 1920s and 1950s it retained the semaphore-era signal bridges. Many of these bridges

Union Switch & Signal's Style S signals displayed aspects by position in daylight and by colored lights in darkness. A lamp illuminated colored lenses in the spectacle from behind. In the early days, railroads had a choice of using traditional oil lamps, or either approach-lit or continuously lit electric lights. Conrail's former Erie Style S signals were approach-lit. *Brian Solomon*

survived for more than 100 years, finally replaced en masse between 2011 and 2014 when CSX re-signaled the route.

Union Switch & Signal Style S

About 1908, Union Switch & Signal revised its electric Style B base-of-mast semaphore mechanism for three-position operation. A few railroads bought three-position Style B signals including Rock Island, which in early 1909 installed them between Davenport and Muscatine, Iowa.

Although derived from the Style B, US&S developed its new Style S mechanism specifically tailored for three-position operation to overcome inadequacies of the older mechanism. Design variations used either alternating or direct current. An improved buffer design better cushioned the arm when it dropped from the vertical to diagonal, and from diagonal to horizontal positions. Early Style S mechanisms used an oil cylinder buffer, while the later models used an air cylinder. The effect of cushioning produced a distinctive two-stage syncopated semaphore arm descent.

American Railway Signaling Principles and Practices described the operation of the air buffer as follows:

> This buffer cushions the signal by vacuum as well as compression. The return of the signal from the 90- to the 45-degree position is accomplished almost entirely by the vacuum created in the top position of the cylinder during the first half of the downward stroke of the piston.

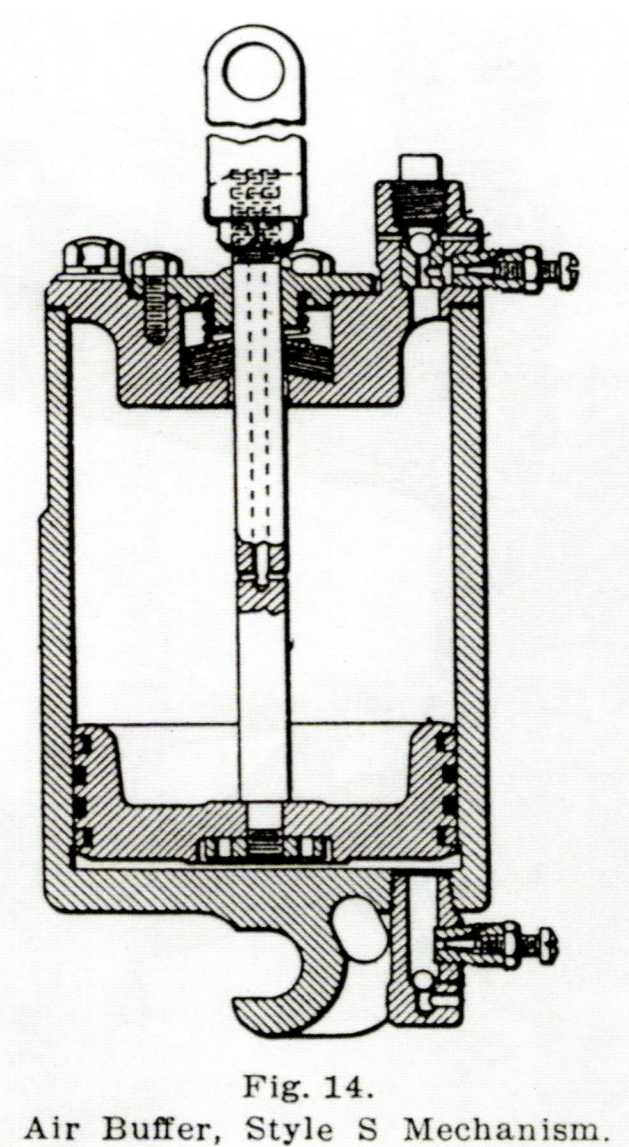

Fig. 14.
Air Buffer, Style S Mechanism.

Among the improvements offered by Union Switch & Signal's Style S semaphore mechanism were its buffers used to cushion the signal blade as it dropped to its more restrictive aspects. Older Style S mechanisms used an oil buffer, while later mechanisms used an air buffer such as that illustrated. *American Railway Signaling Principles and Practices*

The movement from the 45 to the zero degree position is cushioned by the compression created in the bottom portion of the cylinder during the second half of the downward stroke of the piston."

Railroads had a choice of using either electric lamps (which were just coming into vogue when the signal was introduced) or traditional, long-burning oil lamps. Today it might seem incongruous that a railroad would install an electrically operated semaphore with oil lamps, but in the early years of the twentieth century the reliability of oil lamps was established and accepted while electric lights were viewed as a relative novelty and comparatively unreliable. Also, where semaphores operated off battery power, an oil light allowed batteries to last longer while offering redundancy in the event of electrical failure. Where electric lamps were used, railroads had the option of wiring them either for approach lighting or continuous operation.

For about twenty years, the Style S was a preferred type of signal hardware applied to new automatic block installations. Some signals remained in service for decades after more advanced hardware had made the type obsolete. The Style S mechanism could also be used for two-position signals where railroads were anticipating the eventual switch to three-position signals.

Among the railroads that made significant use of the Style S in main line service were: Atlantic Coast Line, Atlanta & West Point, Central of Georgia, Erie (and affiliated lines), Frisco, Missouri-Kansas-Texas, Nickel Plate Road, Norfolk & Western, Santa Fe, Wabash, and Western Maryland.

Erie Railroad Style S Semaphores

Until the early twentieth century, Erie Railroad largely relied on timetable, train order, and manual block systems to protect train movements. It installed its first

On April 16, 1988, Conrail's eastward BUOI (Buffalo, New York, to Oak Island, New Jersey) roared through the Canisteo Valley during a snow squall, passing a vintage Erie Railroad Style S semaphore at Cameron Mills. Erie's investment in Style S signals between 1909 and 1917 was still evident more than 80 years later. One wonders if the hardware installed today will still be active after eight decades of continuous service. *Brian Solomon*

block signals around 1906 using Style B lower quadrants on heavily traveled sections of its New York Division.

Beginning in 1909, Erie made a large investment in Style S semaphores for automatic block service on its Susquehanna Division (Susquehanna, Pennsylvania to Hornell, New York). *The Signal Engineer* reported that Erie commissioned 289 signals on 140 miles of Susquehanna Division double track on December 17, 1910. Erie's average block was 4,959 feet with the maximum block length limited to 7,000 feet.

Significantly, Erie experimented with yellow enameled semaphore blades on its Susquehanna installation. Previous to this, Pennsylvania Railroad had adopted yellow as its standard semaphore color because it deemed red inappropriate since crews would become accustomed to passing a red signal, and that red should always be viewed as a restrictive color.

In 1912, *The Signal Engineer* reported that Erie's choice of yellow was based on sighting, as the railroad's signal engineers believed that yellow was more visible than red under many conditions and was especially advantageous against mountain backdrops while noting specifically that "yellow also offers a better contrast against green foliage." After a trial period, Erie adopted yellow blades as standard, making it one of several railroads that preferred yellow for upper-quadrant semaphore blades.

The success of the Style S on the Susquehanna Division led Erie to invest in Style S semaphores for automatic block service on most of its directional double-track main lines. During the first half of 1912, Erie installed Style S semaphores along 105 miles of its Delaware Division (Port Jervis, New York to Susquehanna, Pennsylvania); 93 miles of its Buffalo Division (Hornell to Buffalo);

Erie Railroad's average automatic block was 4,959 feet long, but specific signal placement varied from block to block to accommodate a variety of considerations, including sighting requirements, highway crossings, and curves. Occasionally, signals for eastward and westward lines were positioned opposite one another. On November 15, 1987, a coal train destined for Bow, New Hampshire, works east on the old Erie at Arkport, New York. *Brian Solomon*

76   Chapter 4

Brand new Susquehanna GE-built Dash8-40Bs lead an eastward freight on the number 2 track east of Canaseraga, New York, on April 30, 1989. A former Erie US&S Style S semaphore protects the westward main track. *Brian Solomon*

and 113 miles of its Cincinnati Division. By the end of the year, it had equipped 157 miles of its main line in Indiana and planned to complete main line signaling over the following two years, but it wasn't until 1918 when Erie installed Style S signals on 35 miles of double track between Lomax and Griffith in western Indiana.

In 1924, the Interstate Commerce Commission reported that Erie and its affiliates had more than 2,000 miles of line protected by automatic block signals. The year was significant, because from that time onward Erie had adopted color light signal hardware for new installations.

Erie's introduction of ABS three-position signals coincided with a change in its rules. Erie signal engineer, M.A. Baird, explained in an article in *Railway Signaling* in May 1925 that "The Erie was one of the first roads to make use of a signal on double track with the current of traffic that could be used in place of the written train order."

In addition to the basic automatic block function, Erie advanced the function of its semaphore system to allow trains to use passing sidings in double-track territory. In this way its dispatchers could prioritize traffic and allow faster trains to overtake slower ones, without the time-consuming and labor-intensive process of transmitting written train orders. Special signals known as telephone train order signals were originally upper-quadrant semaphores with a subsidiary blunt end blade, located on the mast 12 feet below the primary automatic block signal blade. This could be set remotely by the train dispatcher to instruct a train to either "Stop and hold main track," "Take siding," or "Proceed on main track regardless of following superior trains." Designated signals were located at the beginning and ends of purpose-built passing sidings, typically with space for 85 freight cars. Telephones were installed near the signal masts to allow crews to contact the dispatcher for additional instructions.

Upper-Quadrant Semaphores

RULE 296—TELEPHONE TRAIN ORDER SIGNALS

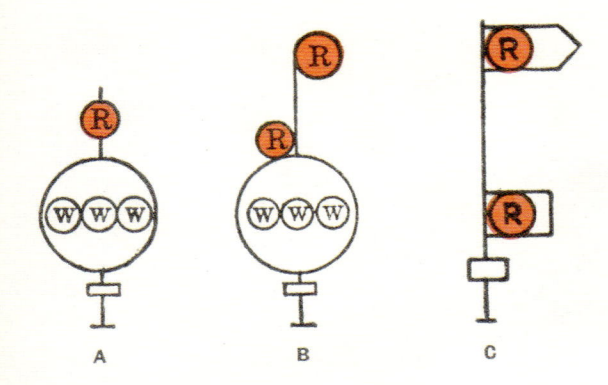

INDICATION: FIGURES "A," "B" AND "C," STOP ON MAIN TRACK AND REPORT FOR INSTRUCTIONS. SEE RULE 509-D.

RULE 297—TELEPHONE TRAIN ORDER SIGNALS

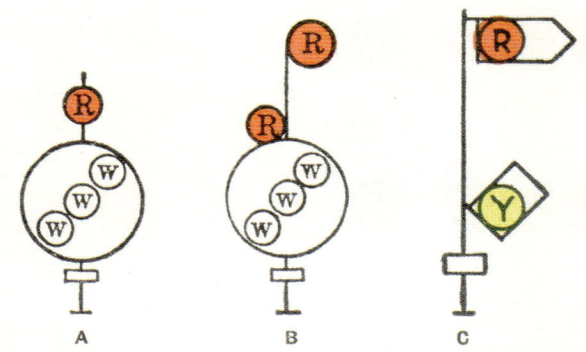

INDICATION: FIGURES "A," "B" AND "C," TAKE SIDING AND WHEN CLEAR OF MAIN TRACK REPORT FOR INSTRUCTIONS. PASSENGER TRAINS WILL REPORT BEFORE PULLING IN SIDING. SEE RULE 509-D.

NOTE: WHERE YELLOW DISC IS PROVIDED SEE RULE 509-C.

◉ Rules for Erie Railroad's Telephone Train Order signals from the company's November 30, 1952, Rules of the Operating Department. *Solomon collection*

◉ Erie Lackawanna 3619 was westbound at Waverly, New York, on July 30, 1972. Signal 255 at the left protected the eastward main train. The top blade is an automatic block signal, the bottom blade (with blunt end) is one of Erie's unusual dispatcher-controlled telephone train order signals. Notice the use of a "dummy mast" to indicate that signals govern the second track to the left of the gantry. *R.R. Richardson, Doug Eisele collection*

78   Chapter 4

Erie was perpetually tight for investment. It introduced telephone train order signals largely as an economy move. Interestingly, Erie's train dispatchers objected to the additional responsibilities for directing train movements, despite the fact that using the signals was simpler than issuing train orders. Yet this set precedents, later adopted by Centralized Traffic Control, which expanded upon the ability of a signaling system to authorize train movements by signal indication (explained in Chapter 5).

Although Erie had switched from the Style S to US&S color light signals for new installations by 1924, it continued to maintain semaphores where they were already in operation. Many of these signals outlasted the Erie itself, which merged in 1960 with its longtime rival Delaware, Lackawanna & Western to form Erie-Lackawanna. Some semaphores survived on the old Erie route in New York State until the mid 2000s, by which time Norfolk Southern had assumed operation of the line. The last was signal 224.2 on the eastward (number 2) track near Endicott, New York, which remained until September 2005 when NS finally retired it and donated it to the Norfolk Southern Museum in Norfolk, Virginia.

The end is nigh: during 1993–1994, in conjunction with conversion from directional double track to single track CTC, Conrail removed Style S semaphores from its former Erie line through the Canisteo Valley east of Hornell, New York. Signal 308 near Rathbone, New York, was out of service at the time of this January 7, 1994, photograph. *Brian Solomon*

Upper-Quadrant Semaphores

General Railway Signal Model 2A

One of the most common types of upper-quadrant semaphore was GRS's Model 2A introduced in 1908. This used the three-position mechanism that was adapted for both top-of-mast and base-of-mast applications. Baltimore & Ohio was the first customer for the Model 2A. It was widely adopted by North American railroads with significant installations surviving in the 2000s.

A GRS advertisement from 1915 extolled the benefits of this signal that included: a simple mechanism substantially built for reliable long life; the mechanism may be directly connected to the signal arm, which reduced the loss of mechanical energy between the motor and arm; simple electrical means were used to hold the signal blade in an upright position and to retard the arm when dropping to caution and stop positions.

Absolute Permissive Block

The General Railway Signal Company was formed in 1904 from the combination of the Pneumatic Signal Company, and Buffalo, New York–based Taylor Signal Company. In 1911, General Railway Signal Company's Sedgwick N. Wight developed an advanced type of automatic block signaling called Absolute Permissive Block system (APB) designed for single-track lines. This used complex relay circuits to provide absolute signal protection between sidings for opposing moves while permitting following moves block to block. This

CSX local freight J-778, worked from Indianapolis to Connersville and return, is near the end of its run having switched a customer on June 9, 1999. The gantry-mounted GRS Model 2A upper-quadrant semaphores at CSX's Indianapolis State Street Yard dated to the early twentieth century. An Indiana Railroad Commission act in 1907 compelled railroads to install block signaling. Many railroads cooperated by installing state-of-the-art ABS signaling. *Hal Reiser*

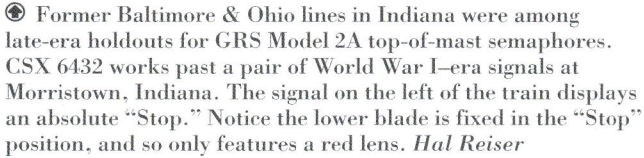

◉ Former Baltimore & Ohio lines in Indiana were among late-era holdouts for GRS Model 2A top-of-mast semaphores. CSX 6432 works past a pair of World War I–era signals at Morristown, Indiana. The signal on the left of the train displays an absolute "Stop." Notice the lower blade is fixed in the "Stop" position, and so only features a red lens. *Hal Reiser*

◉ Near Sandpoint, Idaho, on July 5, 1994, a westward Burlington Northern freight on Montana Rail Link's former Northern Pacific mainline passes semaphores. The signal on the left carries a former Great Northern blade. In this modern context there was no difference in interpretation between a pointed and blunt end semaphore blade. *Brian Solomon*

◉ Northern Pacific's mainlines were largely protected by General Railway Signal upper-quadrant semaphores powered by Model 2A base-of-mast mechanisms. NP was assimilated into Burlington Northern in 1970, and in 1987, Montana Rail Link was created to assume operation of NP mainlines in western Montana and the Idaho panhandle, where many of the old signals survived. An eastward Burlington Northern freight ascends Montana Rail Link's Winston Hill east of Helena, Montana, on November 20, 1988. *John Leopard*

Upper-Quadrant Semaphores 81

Contrasts in technology on the old Monon at Crawfordsville, Indiana: Amtrak's General Electric Genesis diesel-electrics built in the early 1990s passes General Railway Signal Company Model 2A semaphores dating from before World War I. *Chris Guss*

maximized track capacity without requiring additional signal operators, making it especially advantageous for busy single-track lines where it allowed railroads to increase track capacity and improve safe operation while reducing employment.

Although the electrical circuits were fairly complex, the operating principle behind APB signaling was straightforward. When a train passed the home signal at the end of a siding, all of the block signals between that point and the home signal at the next siding for traffic moving in the opposite direction would immediately drop to their most restrictive aspects. As the train moved from block to block, signals behind it would clear in the normal manner, typically giving two-block protection. Thus trains could follow one another safely between sidings.

Absolute signals were used at the ends of sidings (and in some situations at the beginning of sidings) while "Stop and proceed' were used for block protection between sidings. As a result, the APB system featured automatic signals that could display a full "Stop," a situation that prior to this innovation would have been unusual. Many roads used the established semaphore arrangement of blunt-end signals without number plates for absolute signals and pointed-end signals with number plates to display "Stop and proceed." In addition, some lines used marker lamps to reinforce the difference between signals.

Under the basic APB system, block signals were used to provide greater safety, but unless otherwise specified, signals did not authorize train movements. Instead, APB signaling was used in conjunction with an established form of authorization, such as timetable and train order rules. GRS's company history states the first application of the APB system was on Canada's Toronto, Hamilton & Buffalo in 1911. Many early APB installations tended to use GRS hardware, typically Model 2A upper-quadrant semaphores.

◉ In October 2002, at South Raub, Indiana, on CSX's former Monon route, General Railway Signal upper-quadrant semaphore with Model 2A top-of-mast mechanism displays "Clear." In this format, the Model 2A used a simple mechanism connected directly to the signal arm, which was held in place electronically. An interruption to the power supply will cause the signal arm to drop to its most restrictive position by gravity. *Brian Solomon*

◉ Semaphore sunset on CSX Hoosier Sub at milepost 274.7 near Campbellsburg, Indiana, on September 7, 2007. Historically, rules for Monon's GRS Absolute Permissive Block system used absolute signals at the ends of sidings. However, in later years, various changes to operating authority and the means for distinguishing signals obviated the need to observe traditional distinctions offered by semaphore blades. *Scott Lothes*

Upper-Quadrant Semaphores   83

For the better part of a century, General Railway Signal Model 2A semaphores protected CSX's former Monon at Romney, Indiana. Monon decided to install ABS signaling in 1910, and in 1911 beginning with an installation between Hammond and Indianapolis. In 1912, it extended signaling on its north-south route between Monon, Lafayette, and Bloomington, Indiana. (Romney is south of Lafayette.) At the time of this sunset image on November 29, 2007, these former Monon signals were among the last active semaphore block signals in the Midwest. They have since been replaced. *Scott Lothes*

Western Maryland Upper-Quadrant APB

In 1912, Western Maryland suffered several serious collisions, and following an investigation the railroad was advised by the Interstate Commerce Commission to install automatic block protection. At the time, the largely single-track railway was conducting operations using a mix of timetable and train order, and absolute telegraph block (manual block). Over the next three years, the railroad invested in a state-of-the-art Union Switch & Signal scheme using positive block protection siding to siding in a system that facilitated following moves similar in concept to General Railway Signal's APB system.

By the end of 1915, the railroad had protected 92 route-miles and was featured in a US&S advertisement. Signaling was focused on the railroad's busiest section between Hagerstown and Cumberland where it installed 108 ABS signals using US&S Style S three-position, upper-quadrant semaphores with Adams & Westlake lamps and inverted lenses.

Despite the advised red-yellow-green color lens standard, Western Maryland opted for the older red-green-white progression, making it a rare late-era example of a railroad adopting three-position automatic signaling using the obsolete R-G-W progression. A contemporary article in *Railway Signal Engineer* offered this explanation: "White is being used for clear on account of the fact that one of the connecting roads over which the trainmen and enginemen from Western Maryland are likely to operate is still using white."

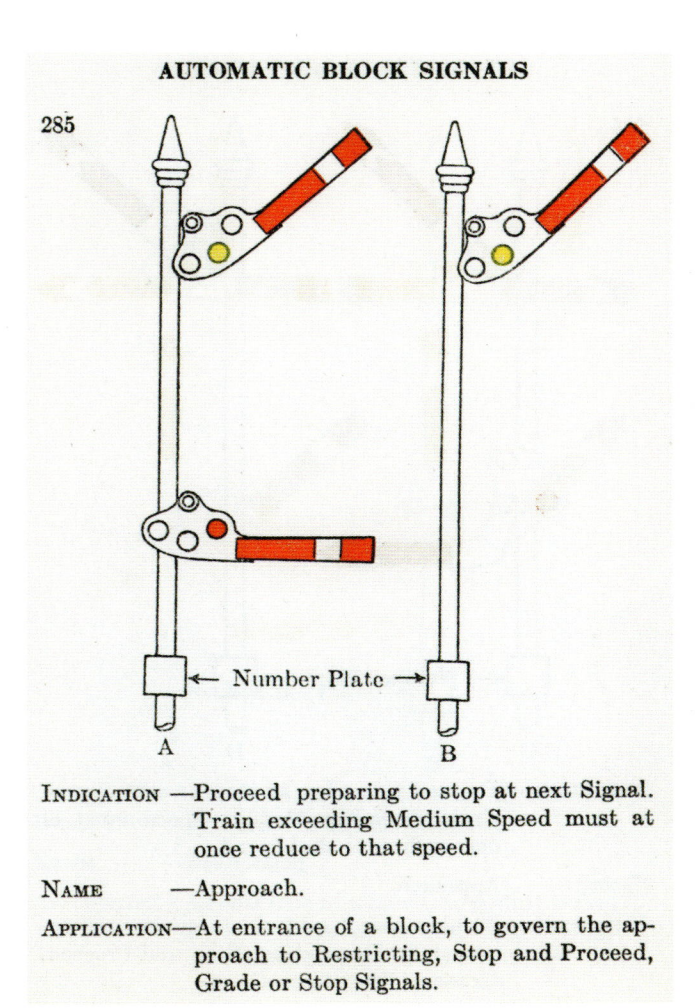

Western Maryland used speed-signaling rules and standard aspects. Its 1939 Rulebook shows the "Medium-Clear" aspect. WM used a US&S absolute permissive block (APB) signal system with Style S semaphores on single track. *Western Maryland*

Western Maryland adopted the three-position semaphore as its standard signal at the time of its original APB installation during 1914–1915. However, with this new signaling, it adopted the old red-green-white color standard (where white was used for "clear," and green for "caution,"), a practice which soon changed to the new red-yellow-green standard. WM's 1939 Rulebook shows the more modern interpretation of the approach aspect. *Western Maryland*

Upper-Quadrant Semaphores 85

This arrangement was relatively short lived and within a few years WM had switched to red-yellow-green for its semaphores.

Lehigh & Hudson River's Absolute Permissive Block

Lehigh & Hudson River (L&HR) was a classic bridge route, and ran from the Maybrook, New York gateway to connections in eastern Pennsylvania. By virtue of these connections, L&HR offered a strategic bypass around the congested New York City area. Traffic flowing to New England from various Pennsylvania routes continued east over New Haven Railroad's Poughkeepsie Bridge route.

By the second decade of the twentieth century, L&HR was experiencing exceptionally heavy traffic. According to articles published in *The Signal Engineer and Railway Age Gazette* in 1914, the railroad was handling an average of 42 trains daily, a dozen of which were

Lehigh & Hudson River 2-8-0 93 leads an afternoon Maybrook, New York, to Allentown, Pennsylvania, freight past pre-World War I automatic semaphores. L&HR used an absolute permissive block system, where the second arm (distinguished by an X on the blade) was raised when the switch was set for passing siding. This three-arm semaphore was an anomaly in L&HR practice since most of its signals had just one or two arms. *Donald W. Furler*

86   Chapter 4

passenger trains, including a circuitous short-lived routing for the Boston–Washington D.C. *Federal Express* designed to avoid New York City. At peak times the railroad was moving as many as 53 trains daily.

To speed operations and improve safety and capacity while reducing employment costs, L&HR installed a state-of-the-art General Railway Signal Company absolute permissive block system using three-position model 2A upper-quadrant semaphores during 1913–1914.

This replaced L&HR's tradition system that relied on time interval separation and train orders. Under its old system, manually operated three-position semaphores displayed "stop" with a horizontal arm and red light; diagonally inclined in the upper quadrant with a green light for its intermediate position; and inclined downward in the lower quadrant with a white light for its least-restrictive position.

Introduction of the new automatic block system resulted in a total restructuring of L&HR's signal rules. It switched from the archaic R-G-W standard to recommended R-Y-G for color night aspects and changed its train order semaphores from the three-position to the two-position variety, while doing away with the interval system for train spacing.

Where ABS automatic signals preceded a train order signal, they served as distant signals. When an operator set a train order signal to "Stop," the next ABS semaphore would display "Caution."

Another feature was the distinctive use of permissive signals to enter sidings. At many sidings a twin-arm signal protected the entrance to the siding to facilitate meets. The lower arm was controlled by the position of the siding switch. When the switch was lined normally (set for the main line), the lower arm was horizontal. When the switch is reversed (lined for the siding) the top arm would drop to horizontal and the lower arm would rise to the 45-degree position, authorizing a train to safely enter the siding.

The theory behind this arrangement was that when trains met, the train on the main line would set the siding switch for the train coming the other way. However, this was not universally applied. In some instances, particularly at lap sidings (where sidings straddled both sides of the main line in a staggered formation to allow multiple meets), absolute (stop and stay) signals were used all around.

Twin-arm, permissive block signals featured a top blade with a pointed end and marked with chevron, while the lower arm had a pointed end but was marked with an *X* in place of the chevron. October 1914 *The Signal Engineer* offers this explanation:

> Where permissive signals are located on ascending grades, where heavy trains if stopped would have difficulty in starting, two-arm signals similar to the entering signals at passing sidings were used to permit a following train to enter an occupied block on a cautionary or restricted indication. As the speed of trains accepting this indication is necessarily slow, and as the responsibility for the same rests on the train proceeding on this indication, there is practically no sacrifice of safety and a considerable advantage in facility. The lower arm of this signal is horizontal when the upper arm is the lead or caution position, but when the upper arm is at stop the lower arm operates to the 45-deg. position indicating block is occupied, proceed with caution.

New Haven Railroad's Left-Handed Signals

In British practice, left-facing semaphores were standard owing to the need to suit left-hand running and the relative position of the engine driver (engineer in American parlance). On most American steam railroads, however, semaphores were right facing (both in the two-position traditional lower quadrant and the later three-position, upper-quadrant configurations). New Haven Railroad was a notable exception. By World War I, New Haven's signal aspects theory conformed to American Railway Association signal code guidelines. Yet, in practice, New Haven signal aspects were among the most unusual in North America.

An early American signaling proponent, New Haven followed many examples set by British practice. In the 1890s, it was an American pioneer in adopting Britain's recently established R-Y-G color progression, and it was early to equip its main lines with block signals, both using variations of manual block (including controlled manual block) and early automatic block in the form of Hall discs (see Chapter 3).

Disc signals weren't always reliable. In 1913, an accident at Warehouse Point, Connecticut, on the busy line from New Haven to Springfield, Massachusetts, had been partially attributed to failure of Hall disc signals.

At the time this photo was taken on June 29, 1987, this signal at Conrail's Readville, Massachusetts, yard was among the last of New Haven Railroad's unusual upper-left-quadrant semaphores still in service. Notice the use of a dummy mast to show that "a track intervenes between the signal and the track governed." The top blade is fixed in the horizontal position, while the lower blade has a top-of-mast mechanism. *Brian Solomon*

This contributed to New Haven re-signaling the line with modern three-position, upper-left-quadrant semaphores. The upper-left arrangement, while common on interurban electric lines, had not been a standard used by steam railroads. Re-signaling was completed by 1915.

New Haven's next big signal project was adapting the left-hand, upper-quadrant semaphores for use on its multiple track electrified lines. The railroad was a high-voltage overhead electrification pioneer and by 1915 it had extended wires from Woodlawn Junction (where it connected with New York Central's line to reach New York's Grand Central Terminal) to New Haven.

Railway Signal Engineer reported that during 1915–1917 New Haven's signal department, under the direction of signal engineer C. H. Morrison, designed and installed a unique style of three-position, upper-left-

88 Chapter 4

◉ On July 19, 1970, former Pennsylvania Railroad GG1 4938 leads Penn-Central train 174 eastbound on the old New Haven Railroad at Bridgeport, Connecticut. New Haven's unusual left-hand, upper-quadrant semaphores and 11,000-volt alternating current electrification date from the second decade of the twentieth century. The dwarf semaphores on the westward tracks facilitated reverse movements. *George W. Kowanski*

◉ New Haven's short-blade, left-hand, upper-quadrant semaphores were a feature on its overhead electrified lines. Semaphores were suspended from the catenary towers, with the mechanisms located above the blades powered by alternating current. These featured adjustable electric lights controlled by signalmen for optimal visibility depending on conditions. By March 1971, New Haven lines were operated by Penn-Central. This former Pennsylvania Railroad GG1 electric is seen near Burr Road Tower in Bridgeport, Connecticut. *George W. Kowanski*

quadrant signal. Signals were suspended from catenary masts and powered by stepped-down, single-phase alternating current from the same power supply used to deliver high-voltage current to electric trains, and used mechanisms powered by single-phase induction motors.

Signals arms were positioned above the tracks they governed, and mechanisms were mounted to the catenary masts with each arm requiring an individual rod-driven mechanism.

Interlocking signals featured twin arms, the top arm spaced 2 feet 11 inches below the mast. At absolute signals, where "Stop and stay" aspects apply, the standard arrangement of signal blades directly over one another applied, and on two-arm automatics, signal arms were staggered in accordance with the standard code.

The size of signal blade was unique to New Haven's application; to fit below the catenary it was necessary to use a short signal blade, which extended just 23 inches

Many of New Haven's "shorty" semaphores survived until the 1980s, when they were finally removed during a re-signaling project that eliminated most line-side intermediate signals in favor of cab-signals. Line-side hardware remained at interlockings where searchlights replaced semaphores. On March 28, 1982, relatively new Amtrak AEM-7 905 leads train 95, the Boston–Washington D.C. *Colonial* at South Norwalk, Connecticut. *George W. Kowanski*

90   Chapter 4

At 12:47 a.m. on September 7, 2007, locomotive headlights of a northward CSX freight illuminate the upper-quadrant single blade at milepost 269 on the Hoosier Sub near Saltillo, Indiana. The code lines and relay box pictured were integral to the signal's operation. *Scott Lothes*

from the spectacle casing and overlapped with the first (red) roundel.

Colored roundels were designed by Corning Glass using high-transmission glass, and each roundel was 8⅜ inches in diameter. The lamp design was unusual. It was larger than those typically used for railway signals and equipped with silver-coated parabolic reflectors with a lamp situated in the center and allowed for an unusually bright light aspect. To improve signal visibility, the bulbs had two settings; a night setting was set at 3.5 volts and the brighter day setting 7.0 volts. The signal brightness was adjusted by signalmen.

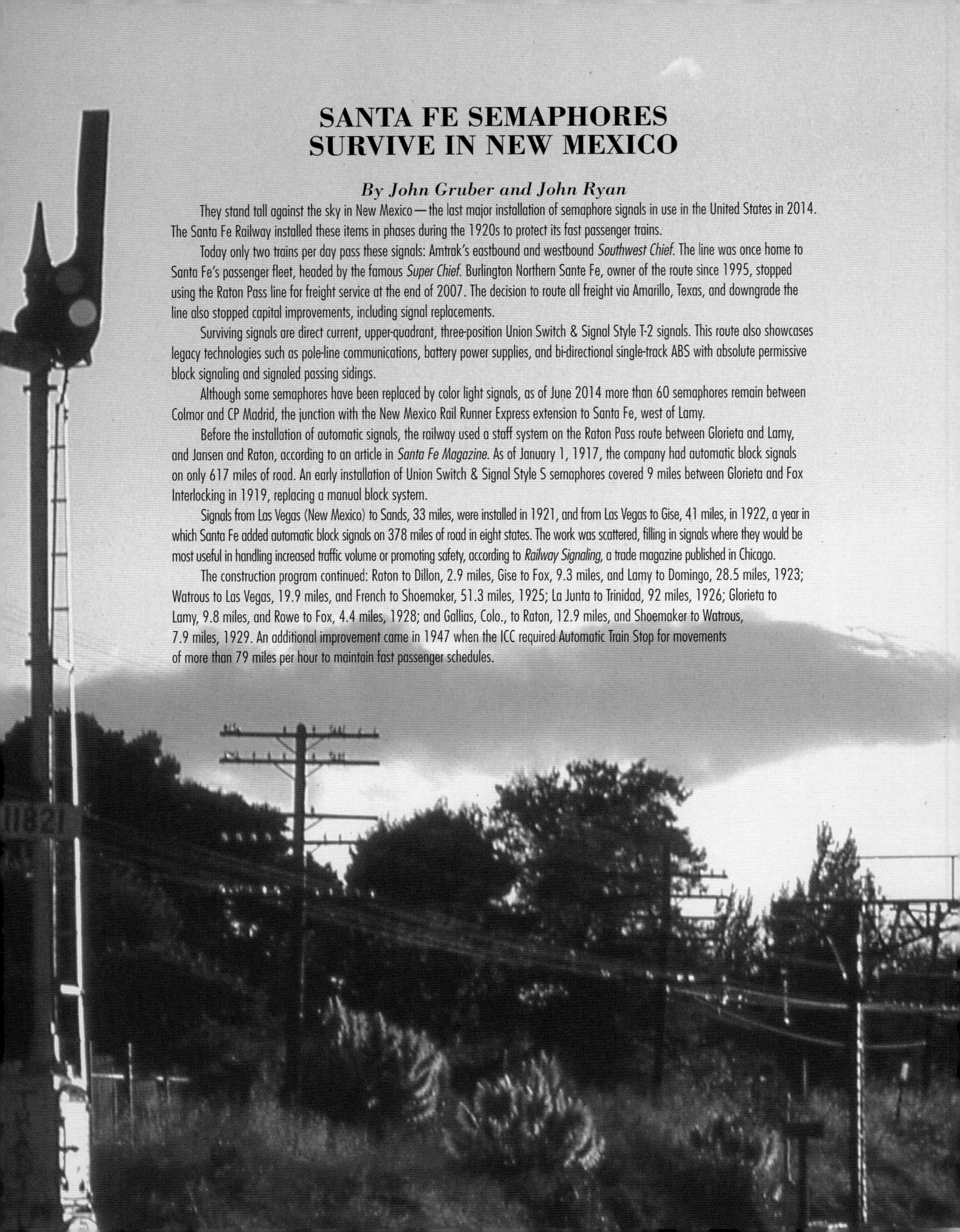

SANTA FE SEMAPHORES SURVIVE IN NEW MEXICO

By John Gruber and John Ryan

They stand tall against the sky in New Mexico — the last major installation of semaphore signals in use in the United States in 2014. The Santa Fe Railway installed these items in phases during the 1920s to protect its fast passenger trains.

Today only two trains per day pass these signals: Amtrak's eastbound and westbound *Southwest Chief*. The line was once home to Santa Fe's passenger fleet, headed by the famous *Super Chief*. Burlington Northern Sante Fe, owner of the route since 1995, stopped using the Raton Pass line for freight service at the end of 2007. The decision to route all freight via Amarillo, Texas, and downgrade the line also stopped capital improvements, including signal replacements.

Surviving signals are direct current, upper-quadrant, three-position Union Switch & Signal Style T-2 signals. This route also showcases legacy technologies such as pole-line communications, battery power supplies, and bi-directional single-track ABS with absolute permissive block signaling and signaled passing sidings.

Although some semaphores have been replaced by color light signals, as of June 2014 more than 60 semaphores remain between Colmor and CP Madrid, the junction with the New Mexico Rail Runner Express extension to Santa Fe, west of Lamy.

Before the installation of automatic signals, the railway used a staff system on the Raton Pass route between Glorieta and Lamy, and Jansen and Raton, according to an article in *Santa Fe Magazine*. As of January 1, 1917, the company had automatic block signals on only 617 miles of road. An early installation of Union Switch & Signal Style S semaphores covered 9 miles between Glorieta and Fox Interlocking in 1919, replacing a manual block system.

Signals from Las Vegas (New Mexico) to Sands, 33 miles, were installed in 1921, and from Las Vegas to Gise, 41 miles, in 1922, a year in which Santa Fe added automatic block signals on 378 miles of road in eight states. The work was scattered, filling in signals where they would be most useful in handling increased traffic volume or promoting safety, according to *Railway Signaling*, a trade magazine published in Chicago.

The construction program continued: Raton to Dillon, 2.9 miles, Gise to Fox, 9.3 miles, and Lamy to Domingo, 28.5 miles, 1923; Watrous to Las Vegas, 19.9 miles, and French to Shoemaker, 51.3 miles, 1925; La Junta to Trinidad, 92 miles, 1926; Glorieta to Lamy, 9.8 miles, and Rowe to Fox, 4.4 miles, 1928; and Gallias, Colo., to Raton, 12.9 miles, and Shoemaker to Watrous, 7.9 miles, 1929. An additional improvement came in 1947 when the ICC required Automatic Train Stop for movements of more than 79 miles per hour to maintain fast passenger schedules.

More information comes from *Railway Signaling* in 1929. New work authorized for 1929 brought the total ABS with block signals up to 5,466 track miles by the end of the year. The shortest through route from Chicago to the Pacific Coast was almost finished — only 57 miles of road remained without signals.

Semaphores were the predominant signal used, except west of Albuquerque, New Mexico, where three-color color light signals were used because of bright desert landscape that required a focused light source, and the fact that alternating current was available or easy to obtain. The majority, almost 62 percent, of the signaling on the AT&SF, was powered by maintenance-intensive wet cell primary batteries.

"Simplified signaling is used throughout in accordance with the established practice on the Santa Fe. Each mast carries only one semaphore arm which operates in three positions in the upper quadrant. All blades are square ended and painted either black or white, depending upon the color and character of the background. A number board is the sole means used to designate signals in the observance of which automatic block signal rules apply," wrote G. K. Thomas, junior assistant signal engineer of the Santa Fe.

These traditions have continued for more than 90 years, a testament to durable mechanical technology. The signals have survived through many changes on the railroad, but face an uncertain future as BNSF seeks to dispose of the corridor between Trinidad, Colorado, and Lamy, New Mexico, and the states of New Mexico and Colorado wrestle with the cost-benefit analysis of assuming financial responsibility for the track, which continues to host only two Amtrak trains per day.

Technological contrasts: modern Amtrak General Electric P42 diesel electric locomotives lead the westward *Southwest Chief* past steam-era Union Switch & Signal Style T-2 upper-quadrant semaphores on the former Santa Fe west of Las Vegas, New Mexico, on November 7, 2010. *John Ryan*

A Santa Fe US&S Semaphore with Style T-2 mechanism displays a "Clear" aspect at Chappelle, New Mexico. Santa Fe had a non-standard color-choice for its semaphore blades, opting to use black, which it deemed best in the austere conditions of the desert and high plains. Former Santa Fe Style T2s are among the last semaphores in ABS service on an American mainline in 2014. *Hal Reiser*

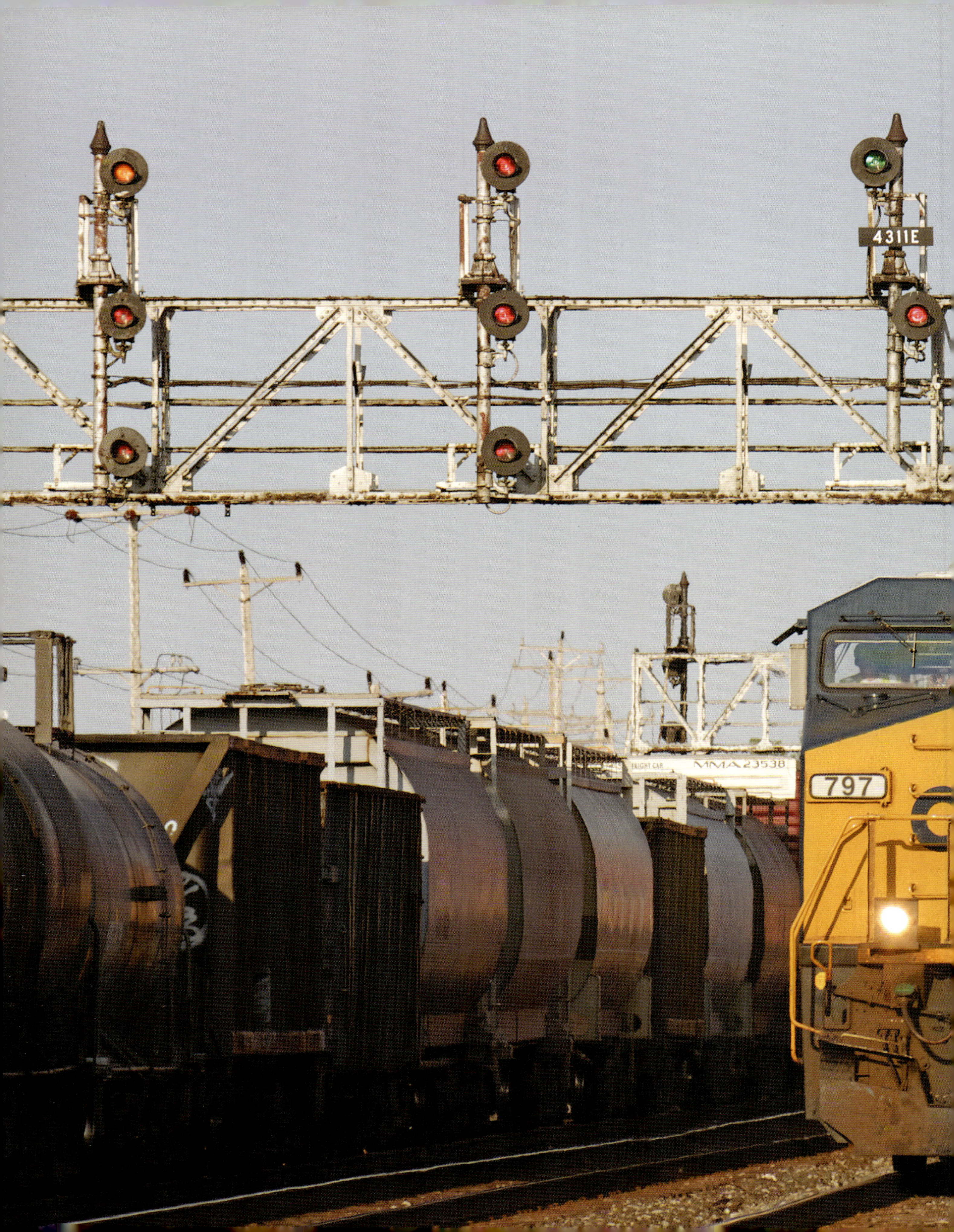

4311E
797
MMA 23538

COLOR LIGHTS 5

Electric Lights and Color Lamps

Historically, semaphore lights used long-burning oil lamps, and while these were adequate for night aspects, they were very dim and thus unsuitable for stand-alone signaling in daylight. Electric lights offered advantages, but in their early days suffered from a variety of deficiencies, so as late as 1912 railroads remained reluctant to adopt light signals for main line operations. Most semaphores continued to use oil lamps until after World War I, and as late as 1924, 30 percent of all ABS signals were dependent on oil lamps.

Electric lighting in its infancy was a far cry from modern lights. In 1910, technology hadn't advanced to produce a small, low-wattage lamp bright enough for long-range daylight signal operation, and electrical supply also posed problems. Before the advent of commercial electricity, remote electric signals were often powered solely by line-side storage batteries, and these needed to be replaced (and re-charged) at regular intervals. The relatively high electrical consumption of early electric lamps made battery-powered light signals impractical for long-term signal applications.

By 1913, significant technological advances in tungsten lamp design had overcome many early objections to the use of daylight electric signals. Optical improvements to lamp design used doublet lenses to focus light from the lamp combined with the use of hoods and/or lens shades to make signal lights more visible in daylight. The use of a dark background further improved sighting by minimizing distracting elements and stray light from immediately behind the signal lamp.

Colored Glass

Among the greatest difficulties that delayed widespread adoption of light signals was a prevailing concern regarding the ability of locomotive crews to clearly distinguish differences between colored light aspects.

Beginning in 1902, William M. Churchill at Corning Glass pioneered high-transmission color glass research. Ultimately this work resulted in the establishment of standard signal glass colors for American signal practice.

By World War I, Churchill was among the most respected in his field, having helped shape signaling practice.

Many of Churchill's conclusions reinforced existing practices, but his research offered clarity as to the choice of signal colors. There was no question that red would remain as the color for stop. In 1915, Churchill wrote in *The Signal Engineer*, "Red is pre-eminently the

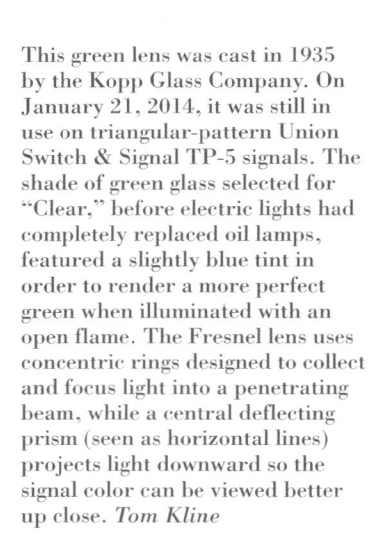

This green lens was cast in 1935 by the Kopp Glass Company. On January 21, 2014, it was still in use on triangular-pattern Union Switch & Signal TP-5 signals. The shade of green glass selected for "Clear," before electric lights had completely replaced oil lamps, featured a slightly blue tint in order to render a more perfect green when illuminated with an open flame. The Fresnel lens uses concentric rings designed to collect and focus light into a penetrating beam, while a central deflecting prism (seen as horizontal lines) projects light downward so the signal color can be viewed better up close. *Tom Kline*

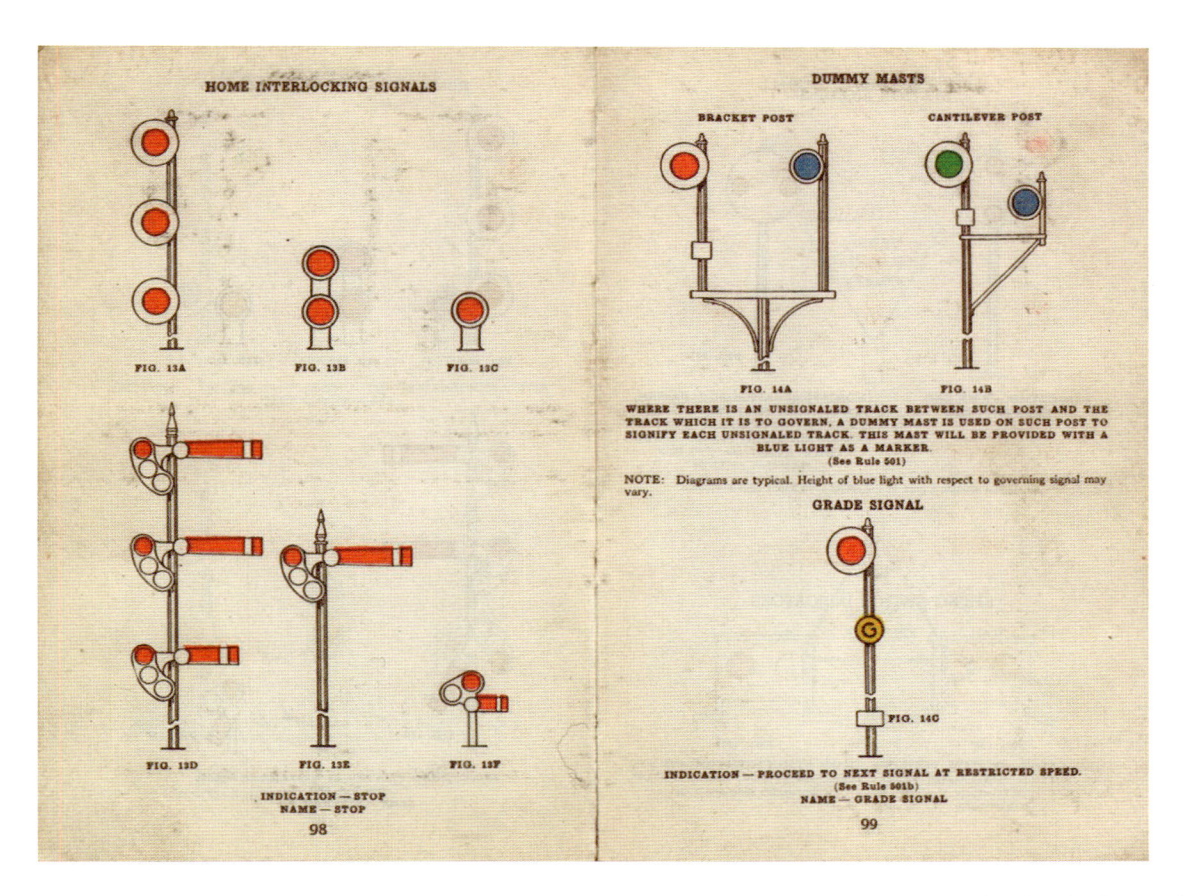

Maine Central's 1952 rulebook used multicolor drawings to illustrate its signal rules. This was one of several railroads that made use of a blue light on a dummy mast when it was necessary to show that there was an unsignaled track between the signal post and the track governed by the signal. *George S. Pitarys collection*

color which throughout nature attracts attention, excites curiosity and arouses action."

Churchill had scientifically determined that after red, green was the next best color that could be clearly distinguished. Yet, by this time, many in the industry were already convinced that red and green were the most effective colors for "stop" and "proceed," so one of the most influential results of Churchill's research was establishing a suitable shade of yellow that could be clearly distinguished from red and appear comparably bright.

Churchill determined that red had an effective range of 3 to 3.5 miles; green from 2.5 to 3 miles; and yellow 1 to 1.5 miles. Of the other colors used for railroad signaling, blue and purple (violet) were found to be visible for less than a mile, which made them impractical for high signals, although both were adopted for other purposes. Blue was used for marker lamps, and purple was substituted for red on some dwarfs. The sixth signal color developed was a pale blue called lunar white that later found use for Restricting aspects and marker lamps on some lines.

On the eve of World War I, American railroads were seriously considering the advantages of light signals. In 1912, *The Signal Engineer* reported on the development of electric light signals, noting that "no system of any kind was ever developed complete and perfect from the start." It continued, "the chief reason for the use of color light signals is that of economy." It was known by that time that light signals were cheaper to maintain and operate than motor semaphores.

Formative Color Light Installations

Pioneering applications of color lights was happening with rapid transit signals in New York and Boston in 1904. Among the earliest extensive color light installations on major railroad was Pennsylvania Railroad's all new Pennsylvania Tunnel & Terminal Company route to New York's Pennsylvania Station that opened in November 1910. This was significant because it was one of the first attempts to reconcile day and night aspects on a steam railroad and it used specially designed hardware supplied by US&S. Signals featured pairs of 40- and 20-watt lamps behind each lens.

Color Lights 97

Other pioneer railway applications for color lights as both day and night signals included: General Railway Signal's installation on a Michigan interurban electric line in 1911 and a commercial installation on the Lehigh Valley Transit interurban in eastern Pennsylvania that began operation in March 1912. Electrified lines were early to embrace color lights since electricity for propulsion could also be used for signals, thus overcoming supply problems facing non-electrified roads in the years before commercial electricity.

Milwaukee Road's famous Pacific extension electrification across 440 miles of line in Montana and Idaho was also the most extensive main line application for light signals at the time of installation in 1915. ABS service began in early 1916 using US&S Model 14 electric light signals in the vertical light arrangement. *Railway Signal Engineer* reported that year, that as installed, these operated using the R-G-W colored aspect progression, making it both a very late example of this antique standard and one of the rare examples of R-G-W for a strictly color light system. Typically, Milwaukee placed eight intermediate block signals between sidings, with the daylight range of signals about 3,000 ft.

Why Color Lights?

The singularity of day and night aspects solved one of the great philosophical debates in American signaling and greatly reduced the number of aspects in the rulebook. Also, color lights were cheaper to install than motor semaphores. The old fears regarding signal failures as a result of burned-out lamps (that could delay trains) were obviated in part by improvements to electrical technology. This included invention of double filament bulbs and relay circuitry that automatically downgraded aspects in the event of bulb failure.

Railway Signal Association Recommendations

In 1917, the Proceedings of the Railway Signal Association offered the following advice on the application of light signals:

First.—Colored and position-light signals, for day and night use, by elimination of all moving parts except the control relays, reduce the number of failures.

Second.—Light signal aspects have greater visibility and range under adverse weather and background conditions than the semaphore, while the close indications compare favorably.

Third.—Light signals give uniform indications at all times. Other types of signals give indication by position in daylight, by color at night, and by both during transition periods. The various aspects of the position-light signal are equal in intensity, range, and visibility.

Fourth.—In general practice, the number of aspects of any one arm of a semaphore is limited to three. With the position-light signal, four distinctive positions may be used, while the number of indications given by colored-light signals is limited only by the colors available.

Fifth.—Where power is available, the cost of operating light signals is less than for operating motor signals.

Sixth.—Current consumption under normal automatic conditions:

Position-light signals: Four 5-watt lamps—20 watts.
One colored light: 35 to 50 watts.

For interlocking signals, consumption is increased depending upon the number of lights displayed, but the ratio holds.

Seventh.—Cost of maintenance of light signals is considerably less than that of motor signals, and, as the colored-light signal has fewer lights to renew, it has an advantage in this respect over the position light signal.

Eighth.—The field for the economical use of light signals is limited, as noted above, to points where power is available. In this field, the light signals have advantages over other types. The position-light signal can be installed at any location where clearance will permit the present standard semaphore to be erected. The colored-light signal can be used in more restricted clearances.

Color Lights Gain Popularity

By the mid-1920s, color light signals of various types were being installed in large numbers by several large railroads and were rapidly becoming the most common type of signal used in North America. By 1924, *Railway Signaling* reported that 3,207 miles of line were protected by color lights, an increase of 1,040 miles over 1923. Semaphores still held the leading position for new installations, with 1,236 miles of line equipped during 1923.

Noteworthy among early color light railroads were; Milwaukee Road with 596 miles protected; Great Northern with 557 miles; Santa Fe with 388 miles; Illinois Central with 310 miles; Burlington with 179 miles; New York Central with 141 miles; and Chesapeake & Ohio with 131 miles.

US&S Color Light Hardware

Among Union Switch & Signal's early commercial color light signals was its Style L signal head, a style designed

This rear view of a US&S color light head on the former Chesapeake & Ohio shows the manufacturer's initials signal casing and the adjustable bracket arrangements used to aim the signal for optimum viewing. *John Leopard*

Color Lights 99

for long-range main line service and available from the World War I era. This featured a linear light arrangement, typically erected vertically with two or three lights, lens centers spaced 12 inches apart. The top light was for "proceed," the middle light for "approach," and the bottom light for "stop." On tangent track it gave a 2,500–4,000 foot range in optimal conditions. The outer lens used a doublet design, 8.5 inches in diameter, while main lamps used 6-volt, 28-watt bulbs with concentrated filaments.

Santa Fe installed Style L heads on its desert lines from western New Mexico, across Arizona, and in southern California between 1922 and 1925. Among these were 114 miles of directional double track between Yampai, Arizona and the crossing of the Colorado River on the Arizona–California line at Topock with 139 signals, and 68.3 miles between Bagdad and Daggett, California in its Needles District with 74 signals installed in 1923.

These were powered by alternating current and used a continuously lit arrangement (yet, concurrent with these installations, was Santa Fe's signaling of lines east of Santa Fe, New Mexico where it used US&S Style T-2 upper-quadrant semaphores, noted in Chapter 4).

Similar in arrangement to the Style L, but with smaller proportions, was the Style N. This was designed for medium-range applications

A pair of Union Switch & Signal Style TP-5 signals provides ABS protection for trains on former Rock Island trackage near Shiro, Texas, today operated as BNSF Railway's Houston Subdivision. Only a few of Rock Island's Depression-era TP-5s remained in regular service at the time of this August 2, 2013, photo. *Tom Kline*

including transit and urban electric railways. This was also a vertically arranged light signal but used a simpler lens design, 5⅜ inches in diameter, spaced 8.5 inches between lens centers. Bulbs were 110 volt, 36 watt with a 1,500–2,500-foot range.

Later types of US&S long-range color lights included its common Style R and Style P signal heads. These both used 8.5-inch lenses, typically in combinations of one, two, and three lights and arranged in a linear pattern. It also offered a triangular cluster color light called Style TR that used the same basic technology as the Style R. Introduced in 1924, the TR offered a more compact signal head and featured lamps closer together, which aided in sighting. It replaced an earlier style of signal made to a similar pattern.

Railroads could choose between vertical or triangular arrangements depending on specific sighting and maintenance requirements. A variation of the triangular configuration was Style TP. Unless otherwise specified by a customer, US&S triangular signals featured green on upper left, yellow on upper right, and red in the bottom position.

Primary differences between Style R/TR and Style P/TP heads was the means used to fix the signal to a mast or signal bridge and methods of adjusting the head for optimal sighting. The Style R/TR featured top and bottom bracket mounts, while the Style P/TP was affixed to top the mast

A Union Switch & Signal Style TP-5 signal lights up the night with its bluish-green aspect. This signal was part of Rock Island's Depression-era modernization program. US&S Style TP-5 inverted triangle displays (yellow is next to green on top, with red on the bottom), with single cobra hood sun visor, were once common on Rock Island. *Tom Kline*

Color Lights

Norfolk Southern 9814 works westward on the former Nickel Plate Road at Dawkins, Indiana, on May 15, 2012. Nickel Plate, like Chesapeake & Ohio, used color light signals with one, two, or three lights per head depending on the specific aspects required at each individual installation. *John Leopard*

using an adjustable socket. Advances in the basic styles was indicated by hyphenated numerical suffixes, thus the Style R-2 was a later variety of the Style R.

US&S long-range color lights tended to use 10-volt, 18-watt double filament lamps powered by AC storage batteries for primary illumination. To conserve power and extend lamp-life, railroads would burn lamps at less than their rated maximum, typically 8 volts, instead of 10.

Examples of Color Lights in Service

Illinois Central simultaneously installed linear and triangular light arrangements. In 1924–1925, *Railway Signaling* reported that IC re-signaled 20 miles of its busy multiple-track line between Gilman and Otto, Illinois, for bi-direction operation using single-head linear Style-R color lights as intermediate ABS signals (with number plates), and vertically-aligned, multiple-head triangular-pattern Style-TRs (without number plates) as absolute signals at interlockings.

Railroads controlled by Cleveland-based entrepreneurs, Oris P. and Mantis J. Van Sweringen—the famous "Van" brothers—included Chesapeake & Ohio, Erie Railroad, and Nickel Plate (New York, Chicago & St. Louis). These lines favored US&S color light arrangements from the mid-1920s onward.

Nickel Plate's Supervisor of Signals, J. H. Oppelt, described in February 1928 *Railway Signaling* an application of US&S color lights for a state-of-the-art APB system his road completed during 1927–1928. This covered 169 miles of main line between Conneaut and Arcadia, Ohio, using 272 US&S Style R-2 color lights, and modern highway grade crossing flashers.

On most railroads, the common light arrangement from top to bottom was green, yellow, and red. Placing

102   Chapter 5

● In the late-1920s, Nickel Plate Road adopted US&S R-2 color lights and APB style control system. The original three-light signal heads used shields 2 feet, 9⅝ inches wide, and 4 feet, 9⅝ inches tall, with single light heads featuring a circular disc-shaped shield 20 inches in diameter. Using an arrangement to give greatest separation between red lights, three-light top heads displayed red in the highest position, while bottom heads displayed red at the bottom. *Chris Guss*

● Nothing lasts forever: at Vauces, Ohio, on August 8, 2012, CSX was preparing to replace traditional Chesapeake & Ohio steam-era US&S color lights and cantilever signal gantries with modern color light hardware mounted on line side masts. Notice that the old signals have individual lens hoods over each lens, while the modern signals use large hoods over all the lenses on a head. *John Leopard*

Color Lights   103

the red lamps at the bottom avoided the possibility of the most restrictive aspect being blocked by snow accumulation. However, Nickel Plate took a non-standard approach with its multiple-head Style R-2 signals. Oppelt explained;

> In order to get the maximum separation between lights on two-unit signals, the top unit is arranged with red at the top, yellow in the center and green at the bottom. The lower unit has yellow at the top, green in the center and red at the bottom. Thus with a maximum of eight feet between red lights, a minimum of six feet is obtained between any combination of lights. The red unit on each signal is equipped with a white backlight which is hooded and gives both day and night indications. Passing trains may thus observe that the signal has assumed the stop position. It is also of value to track workers on single track, as it warns them of the presence of trains in the block.

Nickel Plate's Style R-2s were wired for continuous lighting using 10-volt, 18-watt lamps, while every

On June 3, 2013, a Norfolk Southern freight works the former New York Central Water Level Route at Dunlap, Indiana. Dating from the days of four main tracks, these bracket post gantries traditionally carried semaphores that faced the same direction (rather than in opposite directions as pictured) and governed the two nearest tracks to the left of mast. Central replaced semaphores with color lights and changed operation from directional four track to bi-direction two main tracks. In the Conrail-era, signals on the left-hand (fireman's) side of the gantries were reversed. Steam-era practices that frowned on fireman's side signals were relaxed in modern times. *John Leopard*

104   Chapter 5

A close-up of Norfolk Southern's former New York Central color lights at Dunlap, Indiana, on the evening of June 3, 2013. The signal on the left displays a "clear" (green over red), which in the NORAC rulebook is rule 281, indicating "proceed not exceeding Normal Speed." The signal at right displays "approach." The staggered signal head arrangement is only significant when these signals display red over red, the most restrictive aspect, which indicates "stop and proceed" instead of an absolute "stop."
John Leopard

General Railway Signal Color Light Hardware

GRS's early color light was its vertically arranged Type D signal head, introduced about 1912. These used doublet lenses with cover glasses measuring 8 inches in diameter and illuminated using 10-volt, 40-watt lamps. Features of GRS signal design included individual doors for each lamp at the back of the signal. These were designed to minimize the chance that a door left open might result in stray sunlight causing a phantom clear aspect.

Compared with most US&S signals installed on main lines, GRS's color lights featured a narrower background shield. New Haven, Burlington, Great Northern, Rio Grande, and Southern were among early large users of GRS vertically arranged color lights. Since about 1925, GRS also offered a triangular pattern color light head comparable to US&S's Style-TR, called the Type G. For dwarfs, it offered Type MD and ME signal heads.

Chicago & North Western's Horizontal Color Lights

Chicago & North Western (C&NW) employed a customized variation color light signal head that arranged lights horizontally. These featured individual heads with one to four lamps, with as many as three heads arranged vertically for home signals.

These were first installed on C&NW's busy main line between West Chicago and Elmhurst, Illinois, in 1925. May 1925 *Railway Signaling* featured a detailed article by C&NW's Assistant Signal Engineer R. M. Phinney, who explained C&NW's non-standard horizontal arrangement:

> The color-light signal gives better results if it is not too high above the eye of the engineman and inasmuch as practically all of the lately installed signals of the North Western are on signal bridges, it was very desirable to reduce the height of the signal as much as possible . . . The General Railway Signal Company, therefore, designed a signal with the lights in a horizontal row. This signal is made up of lamp boxes, one to four being used as required.

C&NW color lights were installed to replace Hall discs and three-position semaphores as part of the railroad's effort to increase line capacity. The color

lamp had adjustable resistance to allow for individual adjustment. Chesapeake & Ohio adopted some of the same lighting spacing arrangements as Nickel Plate, although it preferred to mount signal heads on extended cantilever signal gantries for better sighting.

In 1929, Erie Railroad installed state-of-the-art signaling on 106 miles of its main lines between Salamanca, New York and Meadville, Pennsylvania. Here it used US&S Style R color light heads (in the linear arrangement) in automatic block and interlocking service, as was detailed by an article in September 1929, in *Railway Signaling*.

⊕ A westward Chicago & North Western empty hopper train bound for Union Pacific interchange passes Nelson, Illinois, on May 27, 1980. C&NW's individualistic approach to signaling carried over into its color light practice. It opted for horizontally oriented GRS signal heads, typically located on signal bridges above the track governed. *John Leopard*

⊕ A Chicago Metra suburban train at Seeger, Illinois, on Union Pacific's Harvard Subdivision passes a signal bridge with a mix of hardware that reveals the heritage of this route as a former Chicago & North Western line. Only C&NW used color lights in the horizontal pattern in automatic block service. *Chris Guss*

106   Chapter 5

lights used single ten-volt, 20-watt single filament lamps. Phinney elaborated:

> Double filaments were rejected in favor of the light-out relay, which provides a much more reliable reserve. With double filaments it is necessary to hold the resistance, which is in series with the lamps, to a minimum because when one filament burns out the current is cut in two with a corresponding change in voltage drop and the voltage at the lamp increases. If this increase is sufficient to raise the voltage above the rate voltage, the second filament will burn out also. This occurred in the preliminary tests.

Later, C&NW installed GRS Type D color lights in the vertical arrangement on other lines, especially where it wasn't necessary (or deemed ineffective from a cost standpoint) to mount signals on signal bridges. Instead, C&NW's unusual left-handed running resulted in signals being mast-mounted to the left of the tracks they governed.

Searchlights

The Hall Switch & Signal Company, which had been involved in automatic block signaling since the earliest days and had done much of the pioneer technical development of signal practices, made its final contribution to American signaling in 1920 with invention of the searchlight signal. This proved to be the most influential and widely used signal head of the classic period. Technologically this blended elements of semaphore and color-light, while having design similarities to the nineteenth century Hall disc.

The searchlight head is a variation of the color light signal. Instead of using a separate bulb and lens systems for each color light, it features a single white lamp focused through a one-lens system. Key to the searchlight system is a miniature semaphore-like mechanism that changes color aspects by moving small colored filters in front of the lamp that projects the colored light through the lens system creating a bright narrow beam.

The design was made possible by optical equipment advances that enabled an exceptionally bright aspect

Searchlights pierce the fog on BNSF Railway's Aurora Sub at De Soto, Wisconsin, on the morning of October 14, 2013. Among the principle advantages of the searchlight signal is its ability to use a very low-wattage lamp to produce a finely focused beam designed to be sighted from great distance. *Scott Lothes*

with a relatively low-wattage lamp. The signal was advertised to be capable of reaching up to 4,000 feet in good visibility conditions. Searchlight signals have been known to be distinguished as much as two miles away.

The signal light is typically centered in front of a large circumference circular shield that resembles a bullseye leading to a colloquial description of this style of signal head as a "target signal."

The February 11, 1921, issue of *The Railway Gazette* profiled the early Hall searchlight, writing that the signal lamp required precision positioning in a highly polished elliptical reflector to focus light rays. The light was provided by a special lamp with a concentrated double filament, one looped around the other, yet both were centered near the focal point of the reflector. The filaments were designed with one having twice the expected operating life of the other. The secondary filament could be wired either in multiple with the primary filament or controlled via a cut-in relay that would only illuminate it in the event of a failure of the primary filament.

One virtue of the double filament arrangement was that in the event of a primary filament failure, the secondary filament would appear abnormally dim but not completely dark. Thus it would continue to display aspects while providing an alert of its filament failure. Since rulebooks always instructed crews to report imperfectly displayed signals, in event of a dim signal light a signal maintainer could be notified to repair the damaged bulb.

Alternatively, filaments could be wired to provide different levels of illumination depending on conditions, for example giving the signal day and night settings. Various lens formations/combinations could be used depending on the specific situations of the individual signal head. For distant applications, a Fresnel lens using the Toric formation was preferred, while a Spredlite lens (used to diffuse the light rays) was better for situations that demanded close viewing, such as in tight curves.

The Railway Gazette also noted that "The coloured 'roundels' are usually about 1 in. in diameter and 1/16 in. thick, and are made of a specially developed heat-resisting glass, ground and polished in accordance with the American Railway Signal Association specifications."

Santa Fe's signal training course provided this succinct description of the searchlight operating mechanism as used by the railroad:

> [This] is essentially a three-position D.C. type relay having an operating coil (armature) and a permanent magnetic field. The moving element is the armature which rotates approximately 13½ degrees each way from the center position due to the counterweight, putting the red roundel in front of the lamp.
>
> When current is passed through the armature coil in one direction, it rotates the armature against a stop bringing the yellow roundel into the light beam. When current is passed through the armature coil in the opposite direction the green roundel is brought into the light beam.

In the original Hall configuration, the armature positioned red in the middle. As a result, when the signal cleared from yellow to green, the red would flash momentarily.

Searchlights on the Water Level Route

New York Central was the first large railroad to make a large investment in searchlights. It initially installed them on sections of its Water Level Route main line between Syracuse and Buffalo where it replaced relatively new Hall three-position, upper-quadrant semaphores. To prolong bulb life, New York Central reduced the lamp voltage of 10-volt 18-watt incandescent bulbs to 9.5 volts.

A New Standard Signal

Although Hall introduced the searchlight, its production of this modern signal head was brief. By the mid-1920s, the advantages of the searchlight were clearly evident, and Union Switch & Signal bought Hall in 1925 partly for its searchlight designs and patents.

⊃ In the 1920s, New York Central began re-signaling its mainlines east of Buffalo with Hall searchlights. In this view, J1 Hudson 5310 leading train 15, *Ohio State Limited*, overtakes a westward freight on New York Central's Hudson Division near Cold Spring, New York. The staggered signal head arrangement featuring number plates indicate that these are automatic block signals. At the time, New York Central's searchlights featured broader shields. *Donald W. Furler*

⊃ At 5:50 p.m. on October 16, 1980, J.D. Schmid exposed this extreme telephoto view of Southern Pacific's OALAC (Oakland to Los Angeles) against the evening backdrop of the Oakland skyline. SP's US&S searchlights mounted on this signal bridge at Fruitvale, as-built spanned parallel double track mainlines, that connected at this interlocking. This was a vestige of SP's suburban electrification, long gone by 1980. *J.D. Schmid*

Color Lights   109

In North America the searchlight became one of the most common types of modern hardware and was the preferred modern signal on a great many lines with tens of thousands installed across the continent. It was especially popular in the West and in Canada. Searchlights were applied to all varieties of block signaling, as interlocking signals, train order signals, and for other specialized applications. By the 1940s, the searchlight was a symbol for safety and was equated with efficient modern railroading.

The searchlight's bright aspect and low electrical consumption, combined with its compact size and singular viewing point gave it advantages over other types of light signals. Unlike position-light and color-position light signals, it didn't introduce new aspects to the rule book since its aspects were essentially the same as those displayed by other types of color lights hardware. As a result, searchlights could be mixed with other types of color lights or upper-quadrant semaphores without rulebook complications.

Ultimately, variations of the type were manufactured in large numbers both by Union Switch & Signal and General Railway Signal. The superiority of the searchlight made it an ideal replacement for maintenance-intensive semaphores.

Advances to modern color-lights allowed for signals without a moving component, made multiple light color light heads preferable for new installations, and by the 1980s, the searchlight had begun to fall out of favor. Among the problems cited with searchlights were problems associated with stuck mechanisms. These were sometimes caused by gun enthusiasts (vandals) who would shoot at the lights from a distance. Although a great many searchlights have been replaced, this type of signal survives in dwindling numbers in 2014.

Searchlight Hardware

Hall's original searchlight head was described as the Style H, which US&S both continued to manufacture and improve upon. US&S advanced the Hall's design with its

The rear of a Union Switch & Signal H-2 searchlight protecting the siding at Muldoon, Texas, on the former Southern Pacific on April 17, 2014. The H-2 head is identifiable by the bottom hinges on the rear door that opens downward. Visible at the top of the pointed signal housing is the sighting device used by signal maintainers to aim the signal's light beam. *Tom Kline*

On June 6, 1976, Maine Central freight DR-2, led by a pair of General Electric U18Bs, has a clear signal to cross the Canadian National at Danville Junction Maine. This signal authorizing movements over the diamond was controlled by an interlocking machine at the adjacent station. Maine Central was one of a few railroads that used a "green over green" color light aspect for a clear signal. This was a legacy with its origins in lower-quadrant semaphore practice (a twin blade two-position semaphore displayed green over green for clear). *George S. Pitarys*

Style H-2 head, which became one of the most common models and was produced in large numbers for decades. The primary differences between H and H-2 searchlights are with the optical arrangement. Where the H uses a single stepped lens on a short lens extension, the H-2 has a longer head to house a compound lens arrangement with two plain-convex lenses—one mounted on the front of the relay mechanism, and another in a lens barrel extension. (One of complications of the basic searchlight design was that while it can be viewed at exceptionally far distances, the nature of its optical projection can make the aspect difficult to see when viewed from an angle at close range).

The compound lens model had the advantage of being visible over a longer distance than the stepped lens. US&S offered both models simultaneously for decades. While the H-2 was more common, railroads including Erie, Pittsburgh & Lake Erie, and Southern Pacific maintained large installations of H searchlights for years even after more advanced signals were available.

Searchlights on the former Erie Railroad at Jefferson Junction near the Starrucca Viaduct in Lanesboro, Pennsylvania. Among Erie's distinctive signal practices was twin-head absolute searchlights that featured an exaggerated separation between the top and bottom of the searchlight to infer omission of a middle head (used for medium-speed routes). *Brian Solomon*

Color Lights 111

US&S Style H-5 was a later advancement that offered significant improvement over its earlier designs. The signal was designed with a better mechanism for ease of maintenance. This featured a relay mechanism with extra auxiliary contacts that were useful for replacing line side relays. The mechanism was more easily interchangeable and featured plug couplers with a separate light unit. Santa Fe and Wabash were large H-5 customers. This Style can be visually identified by its larger signal housing that featured a squared off peaked top.

◉ Two Union Switch & Signal H-5s stand in profile on January 15, 2014. These protect the north end of the siding at Sealy, Texas, on BNSF's Galveston Subdivision. The shorter signal controls the siding while the taller signal governs movements on the mainline and is situated between the main and siding, which accounts for the mounting arm extending forward to maintain clearance standards. Originally these searchlights were installed as replacements for semaphores, but in this photo they were working their last days pending replacement for new hardware adaptable to Positive Train Control systems. *Tom Kline*

◉ A BNSF local freight works east at East Earlville, Illinois, on April 13, 2010. General Railway Signal searchlights protected movements on this former Chicago, Burlington & Quincy mainline between Aurora and Galesburg, Illinois. Historically, the code line parallel to the tracks carried vital information key to signal operation. Modern signaling systems has dispensed with the need for traditional multiple-tier wooden-pole-supported code lines such as those pictured to the left of the tracks. *John Leopard.*

112   Chapter 5

In the mid-1920s, New York Central's original Hall Searchlights featured large shields and were painted flat black. Later, Central replaced these with more modern General Railway Signal searchlights with a smaller background shield. In August 2010, a westward CSX double-stack train rolls under vintage signals at Depew, New York. *Brian Solomon*

Beginning in 1927, General Railway Signal offered several variations of its compact searchlight. Its original Type S searchlight was soon followed by the Type SA, which was produced as both high signal and a dwarf. A variation using compound lens arrangement was developed later, but GRS didn't offer a separate model to distinguish between its stepped and compound signal variations.

GRS Type SA searchlights were widely used across North America with tens of thousands manufactured. Large customers included: Boston & Maine, Burlington, Canadian National, Canadian Pacific, New York Central, Northern Pacific, and the Rio Grande.

Centralized Traffic Control

In the 1920s, General Railway Signal's Sedgwick N. Wight advanced his absolute permissive block technology into an even more powerful signal control system. His development of Centralized Traffic Control (CTC) successfully combined elements of interlocking

Color Lights

◉ In 1933, General Railway Signal installed a state-of-the-art Centralized Traffic Control machine in Boston & Maine's existing interlocking tower at Waltham, Massachusetts. In its original configuration this controlled five single switches and six crossovers. Although the scope of its control was much reduced in its last years, Waltham outlasted all others in New England and was finally closed in 2013.
Tim Doherty

◉ A professional and conscientious railroader at work: Waltham operator Eddie Bangs observes an inbound MBTA commuter train on October 19, 2008. Bangs worked in towers for 42 years before retiring in 2009.
Tim Doherty

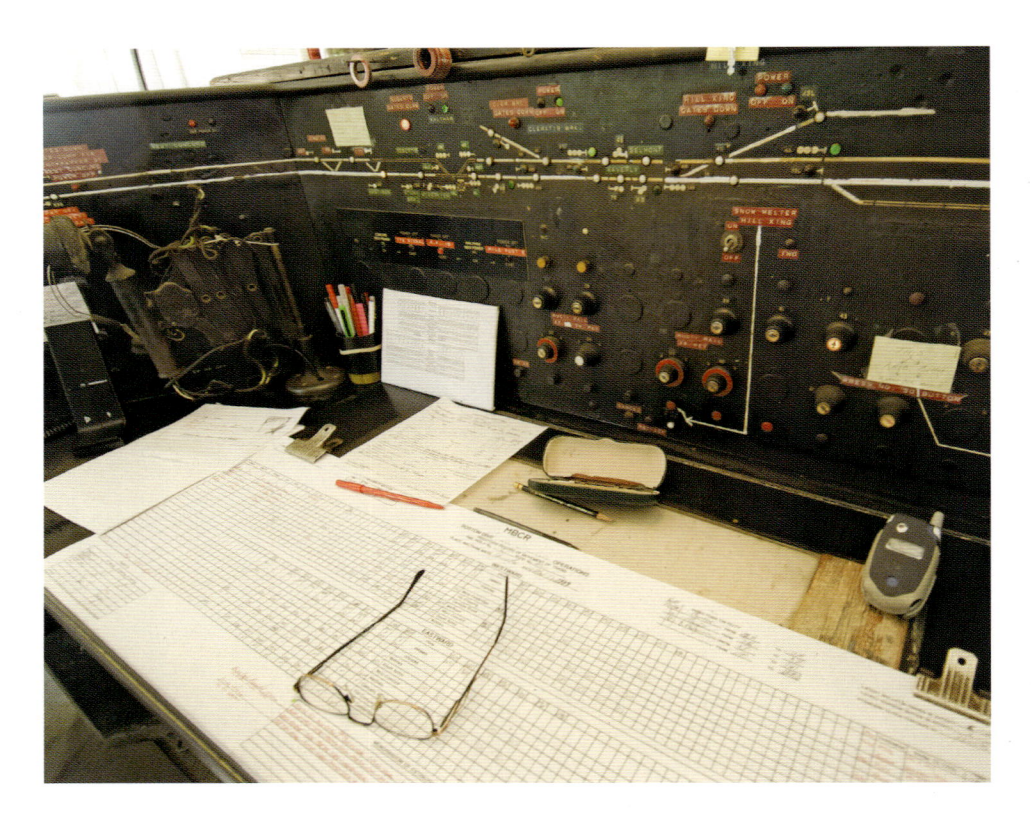

114   Chapter 5

and automatic block signaling using relay logic circuits to provide a single signal operator complete control over line side operations.

Automatic block signal under CTC had almost all the advantages of controlled manual block, automatic block, and interlocking signals combined in one system. By using CTC, a railroad could greatly extend the reach of an interlocking tower over many miles. CTC signaling could be used to increase capacity, ease bottlenecks, reduce transit times, and lower employment costs.

GRS's first CTC installation was on New York Central's Ohio Division between Stanley and Berwick, Ohio, which entered service on July 25, 1927. Union Switch & Signal soon adopted and improved the concept, and by the late 1920s, both manufacturers were building push button signaling networks.

In order to avoid GRS-trademark infringement, the Interstate Commerce Commission developed the generic term Traffic Control System (TCS) to describe a signaling system where signals superseded traditional rules and the trains operated on signal indication without needing paper authority (via timetable or train order). While some railroads adopted TCS terminology, the initials CTC have continued to enjoy widespread usage in the industry and CTC remains the dominant term to describe this style of signal control system, regardless of manufacturer or railroad.

CTC at Work

In its most basic configuration, a CTC system provides an operator with direct control of signals and dispensed

A General Railway Signal Company Traffic Master CTC console served the Cotton Belt at Pine Bluff, Arkansas. Centralized Traffic Control signaling was one of the great labor saving systems of the mid-twentieth century. With CTC, one operator could control switches and signals on hundreds of miles of line. *Tom Kline*

with timetable and train order protocols. In most circumstances, CTC also gives an operator remote control of power switches. By virtue of unifying control, it enabled a lone signal operator to directly communicate operating instructions to train crews without the need for intermediaries. It effectively allowed the combining of jobs performed by dispatcher, operator, and lever man into one position, while giving a lone dispatcher control of many interlockings.

Some railroads were quick to recognize the cost savings afforded by the new system. Yet, union agreements sometimes limited individual railroads' ability to take full advantage of this labor savings tool. Companies such as Pennsylvania Railroad and Reading were required to employ separate dispatchers and CTC machine operators.

Ultimately, Centralized Traffic Control in combination with other technological innovations completely changed

Boston & Maine train director Percy Fonda works the night shift at the tower in Johnsonville, New York, on October 22, 1955. B&M was among the earliest to install Centralized Traffic Control to ease operations on its busy main lines. *Jim Shaughnessy*

the way American railroads moved traffic. Its great flexibility allowed railroads to operate without the constraints of schedules. It improved safety by reducing the chances of human error, specifically the misreading of train orders.

Further technological advancements continued to improve CTC signaling as a tool for remote-control railroading. Early CTC installations were typically short stretches measuring just 30 to 40 miles long and often installed at bottlenecks and where several routes joined together. While it required a large investment, CTC lowered long term operating costs.

Advances such as a push-button automatic route selection system, introduced in 1937, made CTC signaling even more powerful. Gradually, the length of CTC installations grew to encompass whole divisions and enabled railroads to centralize dispatching functions. Railroads installed CTC to replace traditional automatic block signaling as well as controlled manual block and other labor intensive means of train control. It allowed railroads to combine and close towers, manual block stations, and train order stations. It enabled fewer people to move trains, while freeing up track space. After World War II, American railroads made a major investment in CTC style signaling. Since traffic on many lines declined after the war, CTC was used as a cost cutting tool and many postwar CTC projects were combined with track reduction schemes.

The advent of solid-state and micro-electronics and modern communication systems permitted further consolidation of dispatching centers, while expanding the territory over which an individual dispatcher desk has authority. The desire to cut costs accelerated as railroads faced growing wage rates and more intensive competition from highways and other modes.

Between the 1950s and 1970s, passenger traffic declined precipitously. Since freight traffic rarely requires the degree of precision timekeeping desired for passenger services, and CTC signaling obviated the need for tightly scheduled operations, freight railroading evolved new means of operating. While railroads today may advertise train schedules between major terminals and even distribute these schedules to major customers, the times are merely advisory and unlike old employee's timetables, these do not represent operating authority. This change to operating practices is among the reasons that modern long distance passenger trains often have difficulty meeting tightly scheduled public timetables.

Coincident with many new CTC installations was replacement of semaphore signal hardware with new forms of electric light signals, including color light and searchlight styles of hardware. CTC installations with color lights was emblematic of railroad progress from the 1930s to the 1970s and represented a change to signaling akin to the parallel switch from steam to diesel-electric motive power.

Yet, unlike the motive power change, CTC was not universally adopted. Some railroads embraced CTC across their main lines. Other railroads blended CTC with sections controlled by traditional directional double track under rule 251-authority (where trains proceeded on signal indication in the current of traffic). Here CTC islands gave railroads a degree of flexibility with pre-existing double track ABS arrangements.

Often CTC enabled railroads to replace or consolidate towers with centrally located dispatchers directly controlling key interlockings situated between double-track ABS sections. A railroad's operating documents, including employee timetable, specified which system of rules was used over various line segments. On railroads such as Southern Pacific, it was common for routes to variously use sections of 251-territory, traditional ABS signaling with paper authority, interspersed with CTC sections at choke points.

Double track under Rule 261 (where lines were bi-directionally signaled and rules permitting trains to operate in either direction on either track on signal indication) combined with CTC crossovers at regular intervals allows a great degree of flexibility. This is especially valuable where trains operate with greatly varying maximum speeds and with different priorities. A skilled dispatcher can safely weave faster-moving trains around slower trains while keeping the line fluid. Multiple track CTC offers even greater flexibility and capacity.

On some lines, older ABS signals survived in 251-territory, while modern color lights prevailed in CTC territory. Thus older semaphores survived between interlockings, where color lights served at interlockings. Such was the case on the Erie Railroad route, described in Chapter 4, where old Style S signals in ABS service co-existed with various forms of color light for more than 70 years.

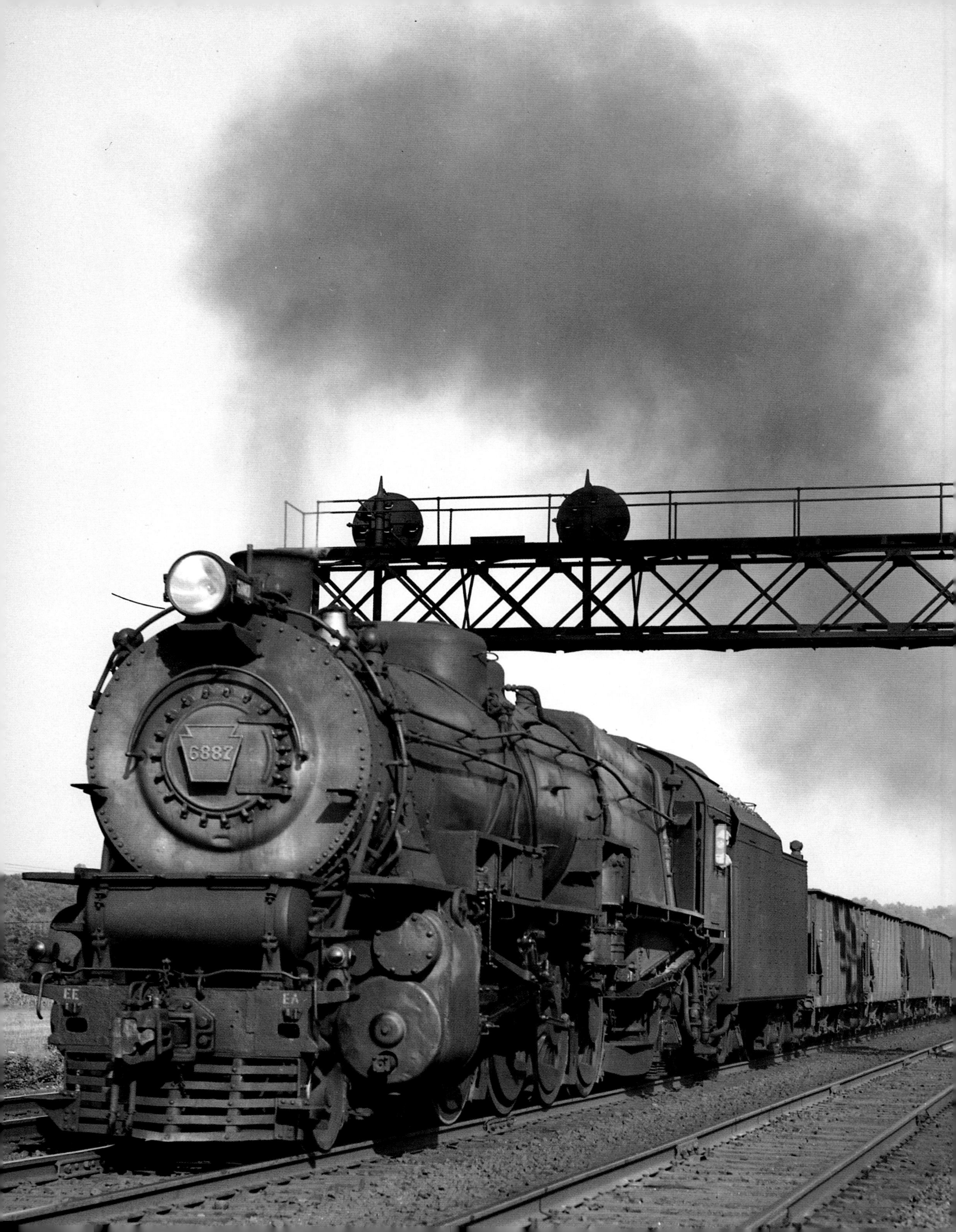
6887

POSITION LIGHT SIGNALS

6

Pennsylvania Railroad Position Light

In the early years of the twentieth century, Pennsylvania Railroad (PRR) was America's largest and busiest railroad. PRR was an empire of its own design, and it tended to do things its own way. The railroad was both a technological trendsetter and a maverick. It was a pioneer for both interlocking and block signal applications and developed its own distinct signaling practices.

Not only did it operate more trains and more route miles than any other railroad, but it had some of the most complex signaling demands as a result of its numerous junctions, multiple track lines, and great variety of traffic using common tracks.

The position light signal was Pennsylvania Railroad's clever hardware solution for two philosophical problems prevalent in American signaling practice at the time of World War I. PRR's signal engineer A. H. Rudd was among the most influential men in early twentieth century North American signal practice. Born in a distinguished family and educated at Yale University, Rudd had worked for a variety of American railway companies and was one of the earliest American members of Britain's Institution of Railway Signal Engineers.

He had enjoyed a guiding influence in the development of many standards embraced by the Railway Signal Association and American Railway Association and was an early proponent

In this classic view of Pennsylvania Railroad's Middle Division, Class M1 4-8-2 number 6887 works west with 115 coal hoppers in tow west of Bailey, Pennsylvania. Position light signals govern train movements in the current of traffic on this busy four train mainline; the two southern tracks for eastward trains, the two northern for westward. These signals were approach lit and displayed the three basic automatic block aspects: "Clear," "Approach," and "Stop and Proceed." *Donald W. Furler.*

119

of the adoption of the three-position, upper-quadrant semaphore and encouraged applications of this signal for speed signaling—a key PRR methodology.

Advances in electric light and electrical technology had paved the way for the development of practical light-based signals. While PRR was among the earliest steam railroads to experiment with color light signaling, it retained serious philosophical concerns with this type of hardware. Also, PRR was among the last large holdouts for the old R-G-W light standard, and only after 1916 did it begin adopting the R-Y-G standard.

Rudd sought means for obtaining the benefits for PRR of both position and light signals. He wanted to obviate the need for separate day and night aspects, eliminate the potential of misreading a signal because of color blindness, and limit the variety of aspects in the company rulebook. Significantly, he also desired a signal head that could offer a distinctive fourth aspect for manual block applications.

In January 1912, *The Signal Engineer* reported that 56,074 miles of line in the United States were protected by manual block, compared with just 20,335 miles of automatic block. While automatic block was on the rise, some railroads, such as PRR, continued to embrace manual block for decades.

Rudd articulated this concern in a paper (reprinted in October 1913 *The Signal Engineer*):

> Signals are divided into four classes—stop, caution, proceed and permissive. . . . The permissive signal is probably needed more on the Pennsylvania than any other road. The great majority of the roads of the country, under manual block, issue a card to enable the engineman to pass a stop signal to enter an occupied block. We give a signal for it. We do not permit a passenger train to enter an occupied block; we do not permit a freight to enter a block occupied by a passenger train; and this practice has been pretty well extended, so that as a general rule on some divisions preference freight is run under absolute block. We have felt it necessary to indicate to the enginemen of fast trains, which are not permitted to accept a permissive signal, a difference between that signal and an ordinary caution signal. It is a stop signal to them, and it must be different from the ordinary caution (distant) signal, which they can accept.

Interestingly, it was Corning Glass's William Churchill that offered Rudd the key to development of the position light. Churchill was the same man who had done much of the pioneering research for high-transmission colored glass that facilitated the advancement of standard glass colors for signal application (and thus made possible the widespread use of color light signals).

In early 1914, Churchill was working to solve problems with electric headlights when he discovered a means of producing a long-range lamp from a small light source by focusing a small wide-angle lens in front of the light source. In 1915, *The Signal Engineer* reported, "In talking the matter with A. H. Rudd . . . it was seen to be altogether practicable to combine these small separate units into rows of lights which would have the effect of the present semaphore arm and would do away with the color scheme altogether."

Over the next year, Rudd refined this concept into a prototype position light system. In its initial configuration, the position light featured ten lamps spaced 18 inches apart and arranged in asymmetrically centered rows allowing for combinations of four lights to mimic the positions of upper-quadrant semaphore arms.

Each lamp was powered by 12-volt 5-watt Mazda lamps that produced 4-candle power. These had three settings and could be adjusted to suit external lighting for the most effective viewing by the nearest signalmen using a light switch in the tower. Typically, lights were set at 11 volts in daylight, and dimmed to 6 volts at twilight and 3 volts at night.

A tombstone-shaped background shield was used to make viewing easier and minimize the possibilities of phantom aspects caused by backlighting. Two heads could be arranged to display every aspect in PRR's rulebook.

The pioneer installation was an experimental arrangement on PRR's recently electrified 11,000-volt AC overhead Philadelphia suburban service on its Main Line between Overbrook and Paoli where semaphores under wire was seen as unadvisable. Signals were arranged in systems of two- and three-block automatic block protection between signal towers.

February 1915 *The Signal Engineer*, quoted Rudd, "This arrangement will eliminate all failures due to moving parts or signals and mechanisms (except the relays) and all chances of freezing or sticking clear." Furthermore, "the scheme solves the colored light problem for night indications completely, by eliminating all colors and establishing signaling by position only."

There was no mistaking Pennsylvania Railroad-style position lights. In November 1998, Conrail SD40-2 helpers work upgrade through Lilly, Pennsylvania. Signals in the distance display "Clear" for both main tracks. Conrail lines largely retained classic PRR signaling under Conrail operation (1976–1998), however, since Norfolk Southern assumed operation of many former PRR mainlines, old hardware has gradually been replaced with color lights. *Brian Solomon*

After a trial period, PRR interviewed its engine crews and found that these men, despite a period of initial skepticism, largely approved of the new design and found the aspects easier to see than semaphores. Despite position light advantages, PRR didn't immediately adopt this new type, and continued to install semaphores at new installations for a few more years.

Notably, in April 1915, after the Overbrook–Paoli installation, *The Railway Gazette* highlighted PRR's re-signaling of its North Philadelphia interlocking, where it replaced traditional two-position, two-arm lower quadrants with three-position, one-arm semaphores.

Improved Position Light

In 1921, following a few years of trials with the four-light tombstone configuration, Rudd reconfigured the lighting arrangement to form a symmetrical pattern based on rows of three lights. This arrangement became standard

Position Light Signals 121

Former Pennsylvania Railroad position light signals on the Main Line near Portage, Pennsylvania, in November 1998. The "G" plate modified the interpretation of a "Stop and Proceed" signal. Historically, on PRR this meant "tonnage freight trains proceed not exceeding 15 miles per hour, expecting to find train in the block, broken rail, obstruction, or switch not properly set." Other types of trains regarded this as strictly a "Stop and Proceed" indication. *Brian Solomon*

and has been in use ever since. The consolidated format required nine lights for the basic signal head, which alone could display the four basic PRR aspects.

Three lights in the horizontal mimicked a semaphore arm at "Stop," three lights in a 45-degree arrangement (from bottom left to top right) mimicked a three-position semaphore at "Caution," and three vertical lights indicated "Proceed." The permissive aspect was three lights in a reverse 45-degree diagonal (top left to bottom right) that was the mirror opposite of "Caution."

In combination with a second head or marker light, the improved position light signal could display 11 aspects in accordance with the standard code. These included a special "Distant switch signal" designed to give advance warning when a main line switch was reversed.

The position light used a specially designed optical system based on Churchill's research. This featured both an interior reflector and an inverted Toric conical lens design intended to provide uniform light distribution, while minimizing the chances of a phantom aspect caused by reflecting stray light from other sources. Key to its high visibility was the yellow shade of light emitted, which was designed to counter the effects of fog and mist.

If this former Pennsylvania Railroad position light signal displayed a diagonal, might it be described as an "amber" at Amber (Cincinnati, Ohio)—a signaling joke, since in British practice the shade of "yellow" used for "caution/approach" is referred to as "amber." *John Leopard*

Position Light Signals 123

124   Chapter 6

◉ A Union Switch & Signal single-head position light dwarf signal used to protect terminal tracks on Norfolk Southern's former Norfolk & Western at Roanoke, Virginia. In later years, N&W used red lamps to display "stop." *Tom Kline*

◐ This position light was photographed at Emporium, Pennsylvania, on September 8, 1997. It is of a type modified to display a pair of red lights in the top horizontal position for "Stop." Notice that extraneous light positions have been blanked out; as a result this signal head cannot display a full "Clear." *Brian Solomon*

◉ This position light pedestal signal was photographed in Pennsylvania on Norfolk Southern's Buffalo Line at the interlocking called CP North Driftwood on Saturday, March 27, 2010. Pedestal signals were low signals capable of displaying faster aspects than a basic position light dwarf. In this view the signal displays "Medium Clear," which applied to a movement from through switch lined from the siding to the main line. *Patrick Yough*

The top head used a circular shield 4 feet 4 inches in diameter with lights spaced 18 inches apart. The signal was designed for the central light to be positioned 24 feet above the base of the signal mast. When used, the bottom head was centered 7 feet below the top head. As it wasn't necessary for this head to show a "Stop" aspect, the lighting arrangement consisted of just seven lamps, the two lamps for the full horizontal row being omitted. Also, in many configurations the bottom head was not equipped with a full shield. A variation was introduced for dwarf signals. These low signals used a different light pattern and a smaller rectangular shield. Here pairs of lights mimicked semaphore three-position dwarfs. Twin-head dwarfs (called pedestal signals) were devised. To minimize confusion with high signals, dwarfs use lunar white lamps in place of fog-piercing amber lamps.

In July 1921 *Railway Signal Engineer*, Rudd cited a variety of advantages to his position-light arrangement, writing:

> A color-blind man can read a position-light accurately. The lights penetrate fogs better than colored lights. Two lights must fail before the signal ceases to be displayed effectively. Four positions *without combination* are available and used, as against three positions of the semaphore and three colors which may be seen distinctively at a distance, and this additional position gives the greatest flexibility.

Position Light Signals 125

Permissive and Restricting Aspects

The unusual "Permissive" reverse diagonal position was adapted for four different cautionary aspects/indications (both alone and in combinations with other lights displayed) in PRR's 1947 rulebook. An unqualified reverse diagonal was given as rule 289, "Permissive-Block" that indicated "Block occupied. For passenger trains, stop. For trains, other than passenger train, proceed prepared to stop short of a train or obstruction, but not exceeding 15 miles per hour. Displayed at the entrance to an occupied manual block when a train, other than passenger, may proceed with caution."

When displayed with a single marker light below, the reverse diagonal indicated Rule 285A "Caution." This specialized aspect was used to protect diverging facing point switches that were not otherwise protected by an interlocking.

The last two permissive aspects were used for "Restricting,"—Rule 290, that indicated, "Proceed at restricted speed, Displayed at an interlocking at the entrance to any route except a high speed or medium speed route. Does not guarantee indefinite progress (track may end or be occupied)." As a high signal this aspect required two heads, the top displaying horizontal row, the bottom the reverse diagonal row. On a single-head dwarf, this was simply two lights displayed in the reverse diagonal position.

Interpretation of the "Restricting" aspect has been altered over the years and in modern times has been more closely defined. In the Ninth Edition NORAC Operating Rules, Rule 290 reads, "Proceed at Restricted Speed until the entire train has cleared all interlocking and spring switches (if signal is an interlocking or CP signal) and the leading wheels have:

1. Passed a more favorable fixed signal, or
2. Entered non-signaled [form D control system—where dispatcher authorizes all movements using form D rules.]"

It must be understood, that under NORAC, and other modern rulebooks, "Restricted Speed" is not a specific operating speed, but a controlled speed meeting a variety of specific requirements, including the ability to stop within one half the range of vision watching for obstructions, trains, improperly set switches, derails and stop signals, as well as broken rails, and not exceeding 20 miles per hour outside interlocking limits and 15 miles per hour within interlocking limits. This is considerably different than an early twentieth century meaning for "Restricted speed," which often meant one half of normal line speed.

As of 2014, Pennsylvania Railroad position lights and signal bridges survive on the northern/western approach to Chicago Union Station. This route served primarily as Milwaukee Road access to Union Station—a legacy that stemmed from the 1870s, when to reach downtown the old Chicago, Milwaukee & St. Paul Railway acquired a half-interest in the Panhandle's circuitous line. *Adam Pizante*

Position lights on Norfolk Southern at Columbus, Ohio; the signal on the left displays "Stop," and on the right the signal displays "Advance Approach." NS's predecessor, Norfolk & Western adapted Pennsylvania Railroad's position light system for its own practice. There were some notable differences: where PRR used a bottom marker light to display "stop and proceed," N&W illuminated single light below the main head at horizontal for an absolute stop and in later years adopted the use of red lights for "Stop" aspects, such as seen here. Another difference is the omission of central lights on top heads. *John Leopard*

Signals for both main tracks on the former Norfolk & Western mainline at Ingleside, West Virginia, display "Approach." The diagonal row of lights emulates an upper-quadrant semaphore arm. In classic position light practice, bottom heads are left unlit unless required and on these signals the bottom heads can only be illuminated with a row of vertical lights. *John Leopard*

Evolution of Position Light Aspects

Position light uses distinctive spacing and lighting patterns designed to give added clarity to aspects, and make it almost impossible to display a false clear because of unusual lighting circumstances. Position aspects are unlikely to be mimicked by non-railroad lights. Adaptation of common semaphore aspects made it easy for enginemen to interpret the signals while minimizing the confusion between the two types of hardware.

After 1921, PRR adopted its position light for most new installations and over the years systematically substituted this style of hardware for older signals as it re-signaled its lines. Yet, by the time PRR merged with New York Central in 1968, the position light had not reached universal application on its lines.

Under Penn-Central and into the Conrail era, lines signaled with position lights were largely maintained with this standard. In more recent times, the position light system, despite its many advantages, has been deemed non-standard, and on many former PRR routes signals have been actively replaced with color light hardware.

The signal has also undergone some evolutionary changes. During the mid-1950s, PRR began introducing red lamps for the outside positions used for the "Stop" aspect while the center light was wired to appear dark. This was applied to help distinguish absolute "Stop" indications. Yet, as of 2014, this change was not universal and some absolute signals still displayed a horizontal row of amber lamps. To accommodate limited speed indications, PRR modified signals governing movements over limited speed routes with the addition of a fixed yellow triangular plate that upgraded medium speed aspects to limited speed. Later, flashing aspects were also added to give limited speed indications.

On the Northeast Corridor, in the 1980s under the administration of Graham Claytor, Amtrak heeded recommendations of the National Transportation Safety Board and began modifying its PRR style signals with colored lights to offer added clarity of aspects.

Although the position light didn't gain universal or even widespread acceptance, several other lines adopted this style of hardware. Notable was PRR's Long Island Rail Road affiliate. Norfolk & Western, also affiliated with PRR in the steam era, was another proponent of the position light, and largely replaced US&S Style S semaphores with modified forms of position lights during the steam era. In the 1920s, Lehigh Valley experimented with the type, but didn't make widespread use of the position light.

Other lines, notably the Erie Railroad, made limited use of position light style hardware in combination with color lights in place of old telephone train order semaphores. In these installations, a position light was displayed below color light block signals. (See Chapter 4 for a description of Erie's unusual signals.)

B&O's Color Position Light

As described in Chapter 3, Baltimore & Ohio's Frank P. J. Patenall was one of the most accomplished signal engineers of his day. No other American signal engineer of his day had a greater breadth of signaling experience. In addition to early patents on the three-position, upper-quadrant semaphore, he had been closely involved in the development of signal approach lighting.

The theory behind his color-position-light (CPL) system embraced many of same principles of Rudd's position light type. Yet it differed in its unique display of aspects. By combining the position and the color of lights it minimizes the potential of a signal being misread, and significantly enabled a single head combined with a marker light to display a full range of speed aspects. Also, the dwarf form of this signal could display all of the aspects of the high signal. Significantly, it was possible for any signal to be wired to show both "Stop" and "Stop and Proceed" aspects, since the marker light, rather than a number plate, could be used as the distinguishing feature between these two important aspects.

CPL Aspects

The signal head offered four basic aspects; "Clear," "Approach," and "Stop," as well as the reverse diagonal used for "Permissive" and "Restricting" aspects. In each

B&O's CPL system is unique by its use of marker lamps with a single head signal to modify aspects for speed signaling rules instead of using multiple color light heads/semaphore blades. The signal at the left displays two green lights in a vertical position with marker lit at top center, which is necessary for a "Clear" aspect. At right, green lights with the top left marker is an "Approach Medium."
Scott Lothes

128   Chapter 6

A single Baltimore & Ohio style CPL head could show all the same aspects as three semaphore blades, while offering more indications. At Deshler, Ohio, CSX 6487 receives a "restricting" aspect in order to reverse on to cars standing on the siding beyond the signal. *Chris Guss*

position, colored lights corresponded to the accepted standard for those aspects; green for "Clear," yellow for "Approach," red for "Stop," and lunar white in the reverse diagonal. Significantly, every aspect with a pair of vertical green lights indicates that the next two blocks are clear; while a diagonal pair of yellow lights always indicates that the next block is clear. Qualifications to the basic aspects are provided by the position of a lone marker lamp.

In this basic form the system is straightforward, but because the arrangement of lights is non-standard it can make direct comparison with other North American signals confusing.

The marker lamps are used in place of multiple signal heads; so instead of displaying aspects on different heads, this signal displays aspects using two lights in position that may be modified by a qualifying marker.

A CPL signal can feature a marker light occupying any one of six lit positions (top left, top center, top right, and bottom left, bottom center, bottom right) as well being left unlit. In its original form the marker light was either a clear lamp, or yellow, depending on its position.

To display an unqualified normal speed "Clear," a CPL signal must display a pair of vertically oriented green lights *plus* the marker light lit in the top center position. Likewise, "Approach" must display a pair of yellow lights in the right hand diagonal with the top center marker light lit. "Stop and Proceed" is displayed with a pair of horizontal red lights and the top center marker light lit. "Stop" is simply two red lights and no marker.

When the marker lamp is positioned in any other position (top left, top right, or the three bottom positions) it changes the speed indication of the basic color position aspects. The progression of indications was arranged to ensure that color position light aspects follow a fail-safe sequence. For example, the basic "Clear" displayed without a marker indicates "Slow Clear,"—the equivalent of a green light on the third head of a color light signal; while a marker lamp directly below the two green lights indicates "Medium Clear"—the equivalent of a green light on the second head of a color light signal. Aspects

Position Light Signals 129

The position of the white marker light was a key to aspects displayed by Baltimore & Ohio's color position light system. This view from January 7, 1997, shows a Canadian Pacific freight running via trackage rights on CSXT near Stateline Tower (on the Illinois-Indiana border); the signal displays "Medium Clear," the most favorable aspect this particular signal can display. A full "Clear" requires the white marker to be lit above the main aspect. *Brian Solomon*

become more restrictive without a marker, so if the lamp burned out, the signal offers a safer indication. This is why the unqualified "Clear" and "Approach" aspects must feature a top white marker light.

Where the CPL aspect progression gets complicated is in its use of marker lamps to the left and right of the primary color lamps. (See diagram in Chapter 2.) In B&O's 1941 Rule Book, a pair of green lights with a yellow marker on the top right indicated "Approach Slow," while a yellow marker bottom right indicated "Medium Approach Slow"—an aspect that had few equivalents in most other U.S. railroad rulebooks.

Patenall designed the system with simplicity in mind, and despite the non-standard appearance of signal aspects, the progression of indications follows the standard code. His intent was to reduce the number of aspects that a locomotive crew needed to memorize while also introducing a distinctive aspect for permissive signals. So while the CPL aspects appear radically different than those offered by more conventional systems, the progression has a more consistent logic within its own parameters and overcame several philosophical incongruities in American signal practice.

An article by Patenall in July 1925 *Railway Signaling* explained:

The basic arguments in favor of the [color-position-light] system are:
1. The day and night indications are the same.
2. With aspects indicating at slow speed, proceed at restricted speed, or proceed, no red lights are displayed; therefore this obviates the necessity of disregarding a stop indication as displayed in conjunction with a proceed indication in [Baltimore & Ohio's] present practice.
3. Instead of trainmen being required 135 diagrams, they will only be required to commit to mind 14 aspects and 6 rules.
4. White upper and lower route markers for high speed and restricted speed routes respectively, indicate clearly which route is set, in conjunction with the block indications displayed.

In addition he believed that the CPL system lowered costs of construction, maintenance, and operation.

In normal operation, most CPL signal heads were approach lit, which reduced their electrical consumption, but made observation of their aspects reliant on a train shunting the track circuit on approach to a signal.

While Patenall's color-position-light system originally featured only 14 high signal aspects, later a number of additional aspects were introduced. Over the years B&O and its successors altered and adapted the aspects displayed by these signals. The August 1, 2001, CSX Transportation Signal Aspect and Indication Rules guide listed 22 different aspects displayed by color-position-light signals.

Over the decades, B&O actively replaced older types of signal hardware with CPL signals, yet never completed the conversion. In addition, B&O affiliates including Chicago & Alton, Baltimore & Ohio Chicago Terminal, and Washington Union Terminal Company adopted CPL hardware.

One unusual adaptation was on the Alton route, which became part of the Gulf, Mobile & Ohio in the 1940s, and Illinois Central Gulf when IC merged with GM&O in 1972. In the 1980s Southern Pacific acquired the Alton between St. Louis and the Chicago area, and in 1996, SP merged with Union Pacific. While these successors continued to use B&O style color-position-light signals, in later years route indications were assigned to aspects displayed by traditional hardware.

CPL Signal Hardware

Baltimore & Ohio was unusual among major railroads in that it didn't use one dominant manufacturer for its automatic block signaling. Since the early years of the twentieth century, B&O had worked with a variety of signaling suppliers. In 1908–1909, it installed semaphores from Federal Signal Company, General Electric, and GRS on various portions of its system. This trend continued when it adopted color-position-light style signaling.

B&O's early CPL signals were manufactured by Hall, and in later years both US&S and GRS supplied B&O with CPL hardware. These companies offered variations of the CPL signal types in their catalogs. For example, in 1937, GRS offered its Type U as a CPL high signal, and two types

A Baltimore & Ohio style dwarf color position light on CSX at Dolton, Illinois, displays "Stop." Notice the marker lights above and above left. The single-head CPL dwarf was capable of displaying all of the aspects offered by a high signal. *Brian Solomon*

Position Light Signals **131**

◉ Signals at night on the former B&O at Carouthers Tunnel in Paw Paw, West Virginia, on the Magnolia cut-off. These two views show before and after the passage of a CSX westward freight on a foggy morning, October 6, 2007. Color position lights show "Clear" on left and "Approach Medium" on right. *Scott Lothes*

◉ A red signal protects the mainline track at the left following the passage of the westward train. This route is bi-directionally signaled on both main tracks giving the railroad greater operating flexibility. *Scott Lothes*

of dwarfs as Types V and Type VA. In the same period, US&S listed both high and dwarf CPLs as its Style G.

Both manufacturers' mast-mounted high signals normally carried the head centered 17 feet above the base. However, the GRS Type U topped at 26 feet 8 inches compared with US&S Style G at 25 feet 5 inches. (The difference was primarily a result of the different final profile at the top of the mast. There were also differences in the base of the signal and mounting arrangements.)

High CPL signals were lit with 13.5-volt 17-watt lamps. GRS offered a choice of hot-spot or spread-light lamps (depending on specific sighting requirements). Also, depending on the desired application, signals could be ordered with various brackets and posts to hold marker lights in any or all of the six positions. At that time, marker lamps were available as a clear lamp (used for most positions) and as a yellow lamp (for right staggered positions).

On the foggy morning of July 30, 2005, an eastward CSX coal drag works the former Baltimore & Ohio Cranberry Grade at Amblersburg, West Virginia. This was one of the sharpest curves on the former B&O mainline and required signals to be positioned at unusually sharp angles for adequate sighting. *Scott Lothes*

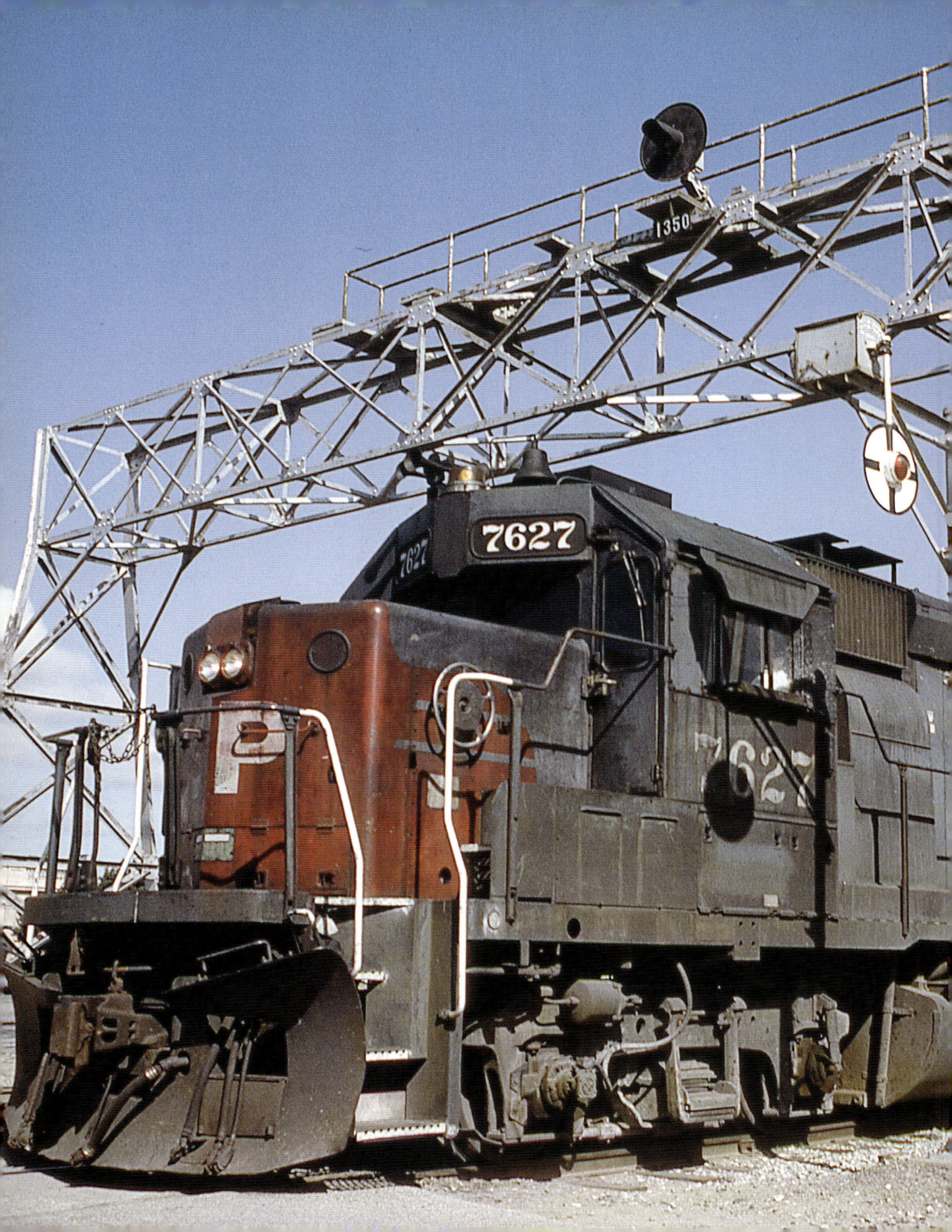
1350
7627
7627
7627

GRADE CROSSING PROTECTION AND UNUSUAL RAILROAD SIGNALS

7

American Grade Crossings

The interface between road and rails has been the point of dangerous collisions since the earliest days of railroading. In the 1830s, a young man and his lady friend crossing the Boston & Worcester tracks in a horse drawn buggy were struck by a train. The pair survived their ordeal, but this incident lead to a public outcry and demands that locomotives ring their bells when approaching and crossing public highways.

The common X-shaped crossbuck was among the early standard signals that emerged in late nineteenth century. Like most grade crossing protection it relied entirely on the compliance of highway traffic.

As both road traffic and railway traffic grew, the potential for collision increased dramatically. The advent of the automobile compounded the problem. Not only did cars travel faster, but the roar of the automotive engine made it more difficult to hear approaching trains. Also, motorists caught up in the thrill of the drive were less likely to heed static crossing signs advising them to "Stop, Look, and Listen."

Efforts to create standardized crossing signals began prior to World War I and tended to be

A Southern Pacific GP40-2 leads a company work train at Gonzales, California, on the Coast Line on April 21, 1994. This wigwag protects a private grade crossing near an SP signal bridge with searchlights protecting the mainline. *Brian Solomon*

A Wisconsin & Southern freight passes wigwag signals on the former Chicago & North Western at Dane, Wisconsin. Once standard grade crossing protection in Wisconsin, when this photo was made in October 2011, Dane was among the last places in the state to feature wigwags, which were finally removed in 2012. *Chris Guss*

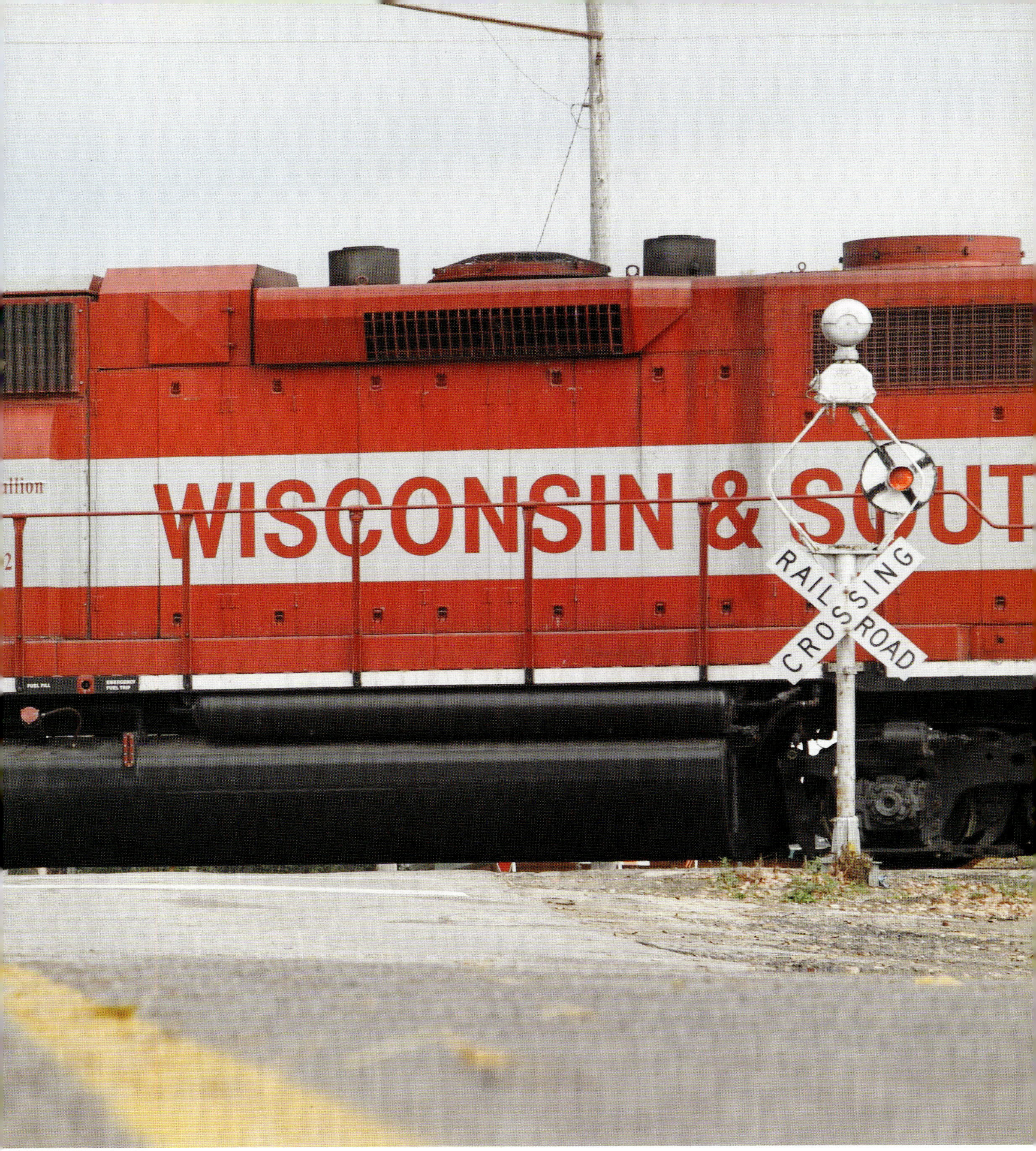
WISCONSIN & SOUT
RAIL ROAD
CROSSING

Railroads manned busy crossings with grade crossing tenders that warned highway traffic when trains were approaching. Delaware & Hudson maintained this classic grade crossing tender's tower where its lines crossed New York Route 155 at Watervliet. *Jim Shaughnessy*

fueled by local or statewide safety campaigns. Yet, by the early 1920s, grade crossing accidents had become epidemic. Furthermore, the traditional method of manning busy grade crossings was becoming ever more expensive as a result of the rising cost of labor. Railroads looking to provide economical crossing protection were keen to embrace modern electrically powered signals in place of manned crossings.

Among the most common types of early grade automatic crossing hardware was the automatic flagman better known as a wigwag. In its classic form this signal offered three forms of warning: a swinging arm, a red lamp, and a bell (which had long been used for audible warning of approaching trains). Various forms of wigwag signals had been sold commercially since before World War I. In 1923, it was adopted by American Railway Association as a standard crossing warning.

In most situations, wigwags were track circuit actuated. When a train entered the circuit, the signal came to life. Its swinging arm and red lamp combined with bell was intended to give motorists ample warning of an approaching train.

The Magnetic Signal Company of Los Angeles was one of the most prolific wigwag manufacturers and for decades this was the preferred type of grade crossing protection for lines across Midwestern and Western states. Although largely a vestige of yesteryear, as of 2014, a few wigwags remain in service in the US.

In a scene repeated countless times, a BNSF Railway freight hits the crossing of South Austin Street at Brenham, Texas, on May 28, 2001, as the aged arm of a wigwag swings to warn motorists of the approaching train. *Tom Kline*

Los Angeles Magnetic Signal Company wigwags were standard grade crossing protection in California for generations. This signal protected a crossing in Santa Cruz. Notice the bell, which would begin clanking when the arm started to swing back and forth. *Brian Solomon*

Another classic accepted form of automatic crossing signal was a metal frame type that featured a revolving stop sign, often accompanied by the ever-familiar crossbucks. This offered a simple and effective warning; when the line was clear, the stop sign turned to face away from the highway; when a train entered the track circuit the stop sign would rotate into place facing highway traffic. The advantage is that motorists were already conditioned to obey stop signs and thus more likely to notice the crossing warning.

Although once common in Minnesota and northern Wisconsin, this type of grade crossing protection lost favor in modern times and has been largely phased out in favor of modern crossing flasher signals. Many of these old signals were the products of The Griswold Signal Company of Minneapolis and have been known simply as Griswolds.

Among the new standards adopted in the 1920s were crossing flashers, designed to emulate the effect of a wigwag. Today, this is the standard form of automated grade crossing protection in the United States. At busy or especially dangerous crossings, flashers are often accompanied by automatic gates that are lowered across the highway.

The Griswold Signal Company manufactured grade crossing signals with rotating stop signs. Looking like a scene from the 1960s, but exposed on September 15, 2000, an LTV mining ore train led by F9A 4210 built for predecessor Erie Mining, approaches Route 1 at Murphy City, Minnesota, where vintage Griswold signal remained in service. By the year 2000 this variety of grade crossing protection was unusual, even in Minnesota, where they were once standard. *Two photos, Hal Reiser*

Grade Crossing Protection and Unusual Railroad Signals 141

On the evening of June 22, 2013, the approach of a BNSF freight on the Galveston Subdivision activates grade crossing signals protecting Peabody Street in Brenham, Texas, to protect motorists from the danger of the approaching train. Today, flashers with crossing gates, such as these produced by Safetran are standard grade crossing protection. *Tom Kline*

Specialized and Unusual Signals
Railroads have had a variety of needs for signals in addition to those commonly used for interlocking, automatic and manual block, and train order applications.

Among the earliest signals were warnings where lines crossed. While in later years railroad crossings with other lines were often interlocked, lightly used lines retained older, non-interlocked hardware. New York

An eastward Santa Fe freight approaches the station and yard at Williams, Arizona, on July 2, 1955. Santa Fe installed unusual train indicator signals to alert employees using a design dating from 1916. These used a US&S Style T dwarf semaphore mechanism to rotate the "train" sign when a train was approaching. *Jim Shaughnessy*

A northward freight on BNSF's Conroe Subdivision at Conroe, Texas, passes a rare former Santa Fe signal called a "Fixed-Blade Distant Signal Approach." This is used to warn of a speed restriction through an interlocked crossing. Signal rules require trains approaching the signal to slow to 20 miles per hour and be prepared to stop short of the next signal that protects the interlocked crossing. The "D" plate indicates a distant signal. *Tom Kline*

The last traditional ball signal in the United States on a Class 1 railroad was located at the crossing of Boston & Maine and Maine Central's Mountain Division at Whitefield, New Hampshire. On July 20, 1974, the crew for B&M's freight G-4 arranges the ball in order to proceed across the Maine Central. *George S. Pitarys*

Central's 1937 Rule Book featured Rule 297, "Stop or proceed as prescribed by time-table. Note—signal may be of Target, Gate, Ball or other type."

In New England, nineteenth century ball signals remained in place for decades after more sophisticated signaling was available. Boston & Maine maintained a variety of ball signal crossings into the 1950s. The last was the crossing with Maine Central at Whitefield, New Hampshire and this signal survived into modern times. The number and/or position of balls specified which track and which direction of travel was authorized to use a crossing. Specific operational instructions were detailed in the company timetable or rulebook.

Other lines, notably secondary routes in New York State, used tilt board style signals, which functioned in a similar way to ball signals. Tilt boards were essentially a manually operated center pivot semaphore that could display one of three positions: horizontal, diagonal, and vertical. Timetable instructions for each specific installation dictated use of the signal and specified interpretation of its positions.

Grade Crossing Protection and Unusual Railroad Signals 145

RAILROAD GRADE CROSSING SIGNALS

Fig. 275 HORIZONTAL
Fig. 276 DIAGONAL
Fig. 277 VERTICAL

Rule 297
STOP OR PROCEED AS PRESCRIBED BY TIME-TABLE.
NOTE   Signal may be of Target, Gate, Ball or other type.

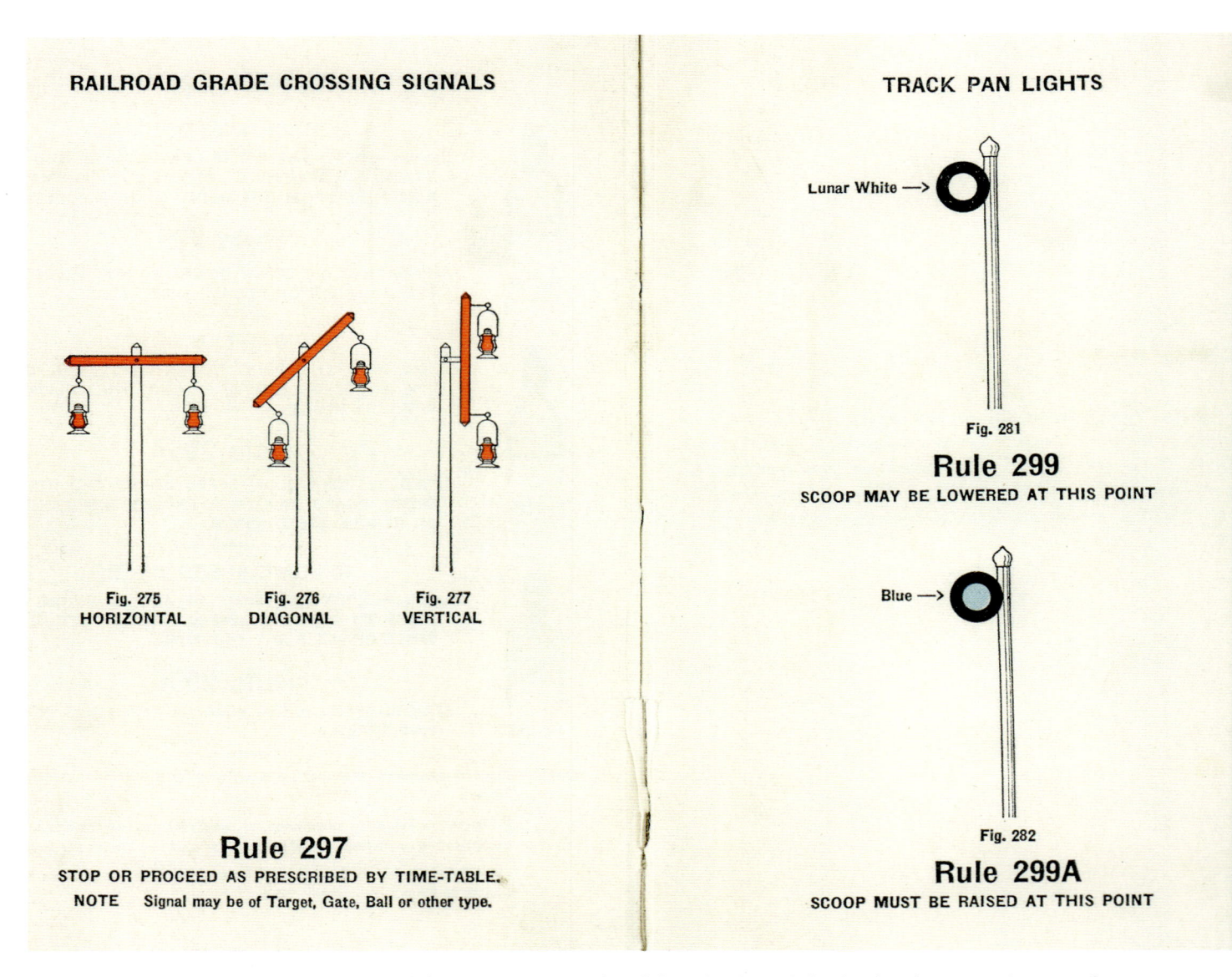

TRACK PAN LIGHTS

Lunar White →

Fig. 281
Rule 299
SCOOP MAY BE LOWERED AT THIS POINT

Blue →

Fig. 282
Rule 299A
SCOOP MUST BE RAISED AT THIS POINT

New York Central System's 1937 Rule Book features instructions for tilt-board style grade level railroad crossings (meaning the crossing of two railway lines), and track pan signals. Rule 299A is an unusual example of a blue color-light signal in operations. More commonly, blue signals (flags and lights) are used to protect workers when working under or between equipment, and are considered some of the most restrictive signals in railroading. *Solomon collection*

"Take Siding" signals were used by a variety of railroads. Erie's Telephone Train Order signals described in Chapter 4 were among the earliest and had some of the most elaborate rules, but other railroads embraced the basic concept. Chesapeake & Ohio, for example, used a position-light style signal to indicate to a train that it should line into a siding.

Safety features such as high-wind detectors and slide-fences offered protection in known hazard areas. Sometimes these actuated special signals, while in other situations, detection equipment was tied into the block system. On the Erie Railroad along its main line in the Canisteo Valley, if slide detectors were actuated they would simply drop the nearest Style S semaphore, warning a train of a problem. Western Pacific had a similar system on its line in California's Feather River Canyon.

Electrified railroads, such as the Pennsylvania, used distinctive signal aspects to instruct electric locomotives to lower pantographs to avoid the end of wire or AC phase breaks. Railroads with track pans (for filling steam

Some lightly used crossings between railroads were protected by simple "tiltboard" signals, where the raised position of the signal indicated which line was clear to use the crossing. These signals were similar to ball signals, where the position or the number of balls granted authority to trains based on the track occupied and/or direction of travel. This tilt board was photographed on September 4, 1987, on Genesee & Wyoming at P&L Junction near Caledonia, New York. *Brian Solomon*

Grade Crossing Protection and Unusual Railroad Signals

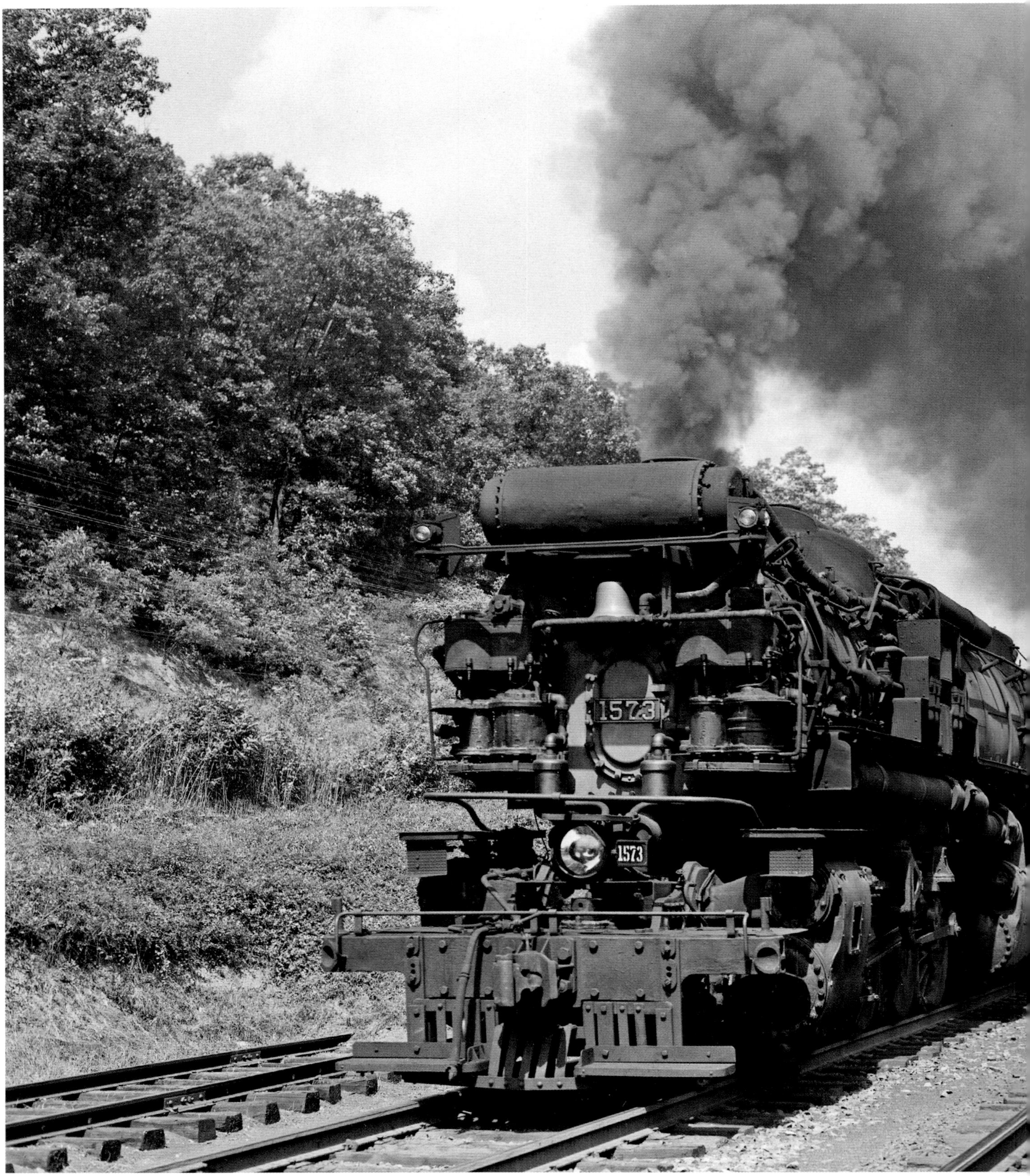
1573
1573

locomotive tenders on the move), including New York Central, used signals to tell crews when to lower and raise water scoops. Failure to raise the scoop at the correct place could be disastrous.

A number of railroads used some form of track occupancy signals; these were tied into track circuits and designed to alert maintenance workers or other line-side employees as when a train was approaching. Southern Pacific used miniature-enclosed semaphores that faced the line.

🟢 A block indicator on Union Pacific at Echo Canyon, Utah, indicates that the block is occupied. These signals were tied into track circuits and used to warn track maintenance crews of approaching trains. *Tom Kline*

🟢 Chesapeake & Ohio "Simple Simon"—officially a Chesapeake-type Class H-7A 2-8-8-2 1573 leads train first 95 with 67 cars near Covington, Virginia. The signal at left features a form of position light that C&O used as a "take siding" signal. When this displayed an X using yellow lights, it indicated rule 294 "train take siding." *Donald W. Furler*

Grade Crossing Protection and Unusual Railroad Signals **149**

ACKNOWLEDGMENTS

My interest in signaling developed from early childhood. A signal's bright yellow over red lights first caught my eye when I was about five, and I captured a photo at dusk of that old searchlight signal on Penn-Central's former New Haven Railroad. Some months later, my father's friend Bill Garrison, then working for Penn-Central, gave us a detailed personal tour of New York's Grand Central Terminal that included a visit to one of its large control towers. Bill saw that I was fascinated by the vast interlocking tower and gave me a copy of New York Central's 1937 Rulebook that has been a treasured possession for many years, and has contributed illustrations to this volume. Over the years, I've studied signal operations on many railways in a score of countries around the world, and I have visited dozens of signal towers, dispatching offices, and signaling centers. My interests led me to author *Railroad Signaling*, published in 2003 by MBI Publishing, which was the precursor to this volume.

In researching *Railroad Signaling*, I scoured many books on signaling practice, as well as signaling journals, railroad instruction manuals, rulebooks, and employee timetables. Yet my detailed research uncovered far more information than was possible to include in just one book. In the intervening years between that book and this one, I've continued my quest for signaling knowledge and answered many questions that I was previously unable to address. For this book, I've focused on the signaling subjects that most intrigued me; including the early Hall disc signals, early semaphore practice, and the development and application of color lights. Again, Bill Garrison quietly led the way, this time by sending me a vintage Hall signal catalog and some other rare signaling literature.

In researching this text, I dug deeper into the archives of signaling literature; I read through dozens of years of railroad trade journals, consulted countless railroad rulebooks, timetables, and other company sources, as well as reviewing my copious notes from earlier efforts.

Many people aided my signaling interest over the years. They directed my quests for information, suggested research sources, provided rare insights on signaling practice, guided me on tours of signal facilities, explained the operation of hardware and signaling systems, and corrected my misinterpretations of signaling practices.

In the 1990s, I would regularly meet with the late "Uncle" Harry Vallas, a retired railroader with seniority on New Haven and Long Island Rail Road lines. His interest in signaling was exceptionally detailed, very specific, and not without deep-seated opinions. Harry proofread my first book, and I regret that Harry passed on before I began this book—his insights would have been invaluable. I've dedicated this volume to Harry!

My father, Richard Jay Solomon, helped in many ways, lending his library, assisting with research, providing photos, and proofreading text. Thanks to my mother Maureen, and my brother Seán for their support. Special thanks to Patrick Yough who generously lent me documents and literature, helped track down technical information, set up interviews, and provided photos; to Harvey Glickenstein who proofread text and supplied insight on New York Central, Pennsylvania, and Reading signaling; to William Keay and John Ryan who assisted with proofreading and fact checking; to Nick Zmijewski at the Railroad Museum of Pennsylvania for valuable help with research and suggestions for photos.

The members of the Irish Railway Record Society allowed me unrestricted use of their library and answered many questions on signal systems around the world. Oliver Doyle, retired from Irish Rail and a signaling expert, organized tours for me, answered many questions, and helped locate rare signaling documents. Doug Eisele inspired my interest in Union Switch & Signal Style S semaphores, forwarded my understanding with signal mechanisms, and facilitated visits to railroads in New York and Pennsylvania. John Gruber assisted with travel, research, and writing, and opened many doors for me over the years. My late friend Robert A. Buck of Warren, Massachusetts, also opened many doors, provided lots of research materials, and encouraged my interest in railroads. Chris Guss provided recent tours of Chicagoland railroading, lent photographic support, made many valuable connections, and supplied caption information. Otto Vondrak helped in many ways, including finding images of the New York, Westchester & Boston signaling.

Thanks to the many railroaders, industry professionals, photographers, and signaling enthusiasts that have facilitated my interest over the years, supplied research materials, answered questions, and/or traveled with me over the years, including; Mike Abalos, Howard Ande, F.L. Becht, Marshall Beecher, Dan Bigda, Scott Bontz, Joe Burgess, Kenneth Buck, Russell Buck, Dave Burton, Colm O' Callaghan, Paul Carver, Tom Carver, Mike Danneman, Tom Danneman, Tim Doherty, Donal Flynn, Mike Gardner, Paul Goewey, Tony Gray, Dick Gruber, Don Gulbrandsen, John Hankey, David Hegarty, Brad Hellman, Tim Hensch, Mark Hemphill, Mark Hodge, Gerald Hook, Al Goff, T.S. Hoover, Brian Jennison, Danny Johnson, Eric Johnson, Blair Kooistra, George W. Kowanski, Dennis LeBeau, Bill Linley, Don Marson, Norman McAdams, Denis McCabe, Joe McMillan, William D. Middleton, David Monte Verde, Vic Neves, Mel Patrick, John E. Pickett, G.S. Pitarys, Brian Plant, Jeff Power, Rich Reed, Hal Reiser, Jon Roma, Pete Ruesch, Brian Rutherford, Dean Sauvola, J.D. Schmid, Jim Shaughnessy, Jim Sinclair, Hassard Stacpoole, Carl Swanson, Dave Stanley, David Swirk, Charles R. Tipton, Jr., M. Ross Valentine, Kevin Walker, Ian Walshe, Matthew Wronski, and Walter Zullig.

A special mention is in order to all the photographers who supplied images and helped with captioning, each of whom is credited with their photographs.

Thanks to Steve Casper, Elizabeth Noll, Dennis Pernu, and everyone at Voyageur Press for their help in the editing, designing, and marketing of this book.

Hundreds of sources have been consulted, and every effort has been made to provide correct and accurate information and the highest quality photographs. Ideally a book would be entirely free from inaccuracies, and it is my hope that this book is as accurate and up to date as possible. In some situations conflicting data and reports have put absolute accuracy in question. In these cases I have tried to qualify data accordingly. Errors, if they appear, are my own and not those of the many specialists that have assisted me. I hope that everyone who holds this book enjoys it and learns something new about American Railroad signaling!

Brian Solomon, June 2014.

BIBLIOGRAPHY

Books

—*Elements of Railway Signaling.* (GRS Co., "A Half-Century of Signaling Progress 1904–1954"). Rochester, NY, 1979.

—*History of General Railway Signal Company,* Rochester, NY, 1979.

—*Tyer's Block Telegraph and Electric Locking Signals,* Fifth Edition. London, 1874.

Aitken, John. *Modern Train Signalling on British Railways.* Glasgow, UK, no date.

Audel, Theo. *Audel's New Electric Library, Vol VIII.* New York, 1930.

Bailey, Colin. *European Railway Signalling.* London, 1995.

Beaver, Roy C. *The Bessemer And Lake Erie Railroad 1869–1969,* San Marino, Calif., 1969.

Blythe, Richard. *Danger Ahead.* London, 1951.

Brignano, Mary and Hax McCullough. *The Search for Safety.* American Standard, 1981.

Burgess, George, H., and Miles C. Kennedy, *Centennial History of the Pennsylvania Railroad.* Philadelphia, 1949.

Cardini, A. *Multiple Aspect Signalling (British Practice).* Reading, UK, 1963.

Casey, Robert J. and W.A.S. Douglas. *The Lackawanna Story.* New York, 1951.

Challis, W.H. *Principles of the Layout of Signals (British Practice).* Reading, UK, 1960.

Currie, J.R.L. *The Runaway Train, Armagh 1889.* Newton Abbot, UK, 1973.

Doyle, Oliver and Stephen Hirsch. *Railways in Ireland 1834–1984.* Dublin, 1983.

Droege, John A. *Passenger Terminals and Trains.* New York, 1916.

Farrington, Jr., S. Kip. *Railroading from the Head End.* New York, 1943.

Farrington, Jr., S. Kip. *Railroads at War.* New York, 1944.

Farrington, Jr., S. Kip. *Railroading from the Rear End.* New York, 1946.

Farrington, Jr., S. Kip. *Railroads of Today.* New York, 1949.

Farrington, Jr., S. Kip. *Railroading the Modern Way.* New York, 1951.

Farrington, Jr., S. Kip. *Railroads of the Hour.* New York, 1958.

Hall, Stanley. *Danger Signals.* Surrey, UK, 1987.

Kichenside, G. M. and Alan Willaims, *British Railway Signalling, Third Edition,* Surray, UK, 1975.

Nock, O.S. *Fifty Years of Railway Signalling.* London, 1962.

Pigg, James. *Railway Block Signalling.* London, no date [1900?]

Phillips, Jr., Edmund J. *Railroad Operation and Railway Signaling.* New York, 1942.

Protheroe, Ernest. *The Railways of the World.* London, no date [1920?].

Raymond, William G. Raymond, revised by Henry E. Riggs and Walter C. Sadler. *The Elements of Railroad Engineering, Fifth Edition.* New York, 1937.

Reed, Robert C., *Train Wrecks.* New York, 1968.

Rolt, L.T.C. *Red for Danger.* London, 1955.

Semmens, Peter. *Railway Disasters of the World.* Sparkford, Nr. Yeovil, Somerset, UK, 1994.

Signor, John R. *Donner Pass: Southern Pacific's Sierra Crossing.* San Marino, Calif. 1985.

Solomon, Brian. *The American Steam Locomotive.* Osceola, Wis., 1998.

————.*Railroad Stations.* New York, 1998.

————.*Railroad Signaling.* St. Paul, Mn., 2003.

————.*Burlington Northern Santa Fe Railway.* St. Paul, Mn., 2005.

————.*CSX.* St. Paul, Mn., 2005.

————.*Railroads of Pennsylvania.* Voyageur Press. Minneapolis, Mn., 2008.

————.*North American Railroad—the Illustrated Encyclopedia.* Voyageur Press. Minneapolis, Mn., 2012.

Solomon, Brian and Mike Schafer. *New York Central Railroad.* Osceola, Wis., 1999.

Such, W. H. *Principles of Interlocking (British Practice)* . Reading, UK, 1963.

Such, W. H. *Mechanical and Electrical Interlocking (British Practice).* Reading, UK, 1963.

Talbot, F. A. *Railway Wonders of the World, Volumes 1 & 2.* London, 1914.

Thompson, Slason. *The Railway Library—1912.* Chicago, 1913.

Vanns, Michael A. *Signalling in the Age of Steam.* Surray, UK 1995.

Walker, Mike. *Steam Powered Video's Comprehensive Railroad Atlas of North America—North East U.S.A.* Steam Powered Publishing. Feaversham, Kent, UK, 1993.
————.*California and Nevada.* Feaversham, Kent, UK, 1996.
————.*Great Lakes West.* Feaversham, Kent, UK, 1996.
————.*Great Lakes East.* Feaversham, Kent, UK, 1997.
————.*Pacific Northwest.* Feaversham, Kent, UK, 1997.
————.*Appalachia and Piedmont.* Feaversham, Kent, UK, 1997.
————.*New England & Maritime Canada.* Feaversham, Kent, UK, 1999.
————.*Southeast.* Feaversham, Kent, UK, 1999.
————.*Mountain Plains.* Feaversham, Kent, UK, 2000.
————.*Texas.* Feaversham, Kent, UK, 2001.
————.*Southern States.* Feaversham, Kent, UK, 2001.
Winchester, Clarence. *Railway Wonders of the World, Volumes 1 & 2.* London, 1935.

Periodicals

B&M Bulletin, Woburn, Massachusetts
Home Signal, Champaign, Illinois.
Jane's World Railways. London.
Journal of the Irish Railway Record Society.
Locomotive & Railway Preservation. Waukesha, Wis. [no longer published]
Modern Railways. Surrey, United Kingdom.
Rail. Peterborough, United Kingdom.
RailNews. Waukesha, Wis. [no longer published]
Railroad History, formerly *Railway and Locomotive Historical Society Bulletin.* Boston, Mass.
Railway Age, Chicago and New York.
The Railway Gazette, London.
Railway Signaling and Communications, formerly *The Railway Signal Engineer*, see *Railway Signaling.* Chicago and New York.
Official Guide to the Railways. New York
Today's Railways. Sheffield, United Kingdom.
Thomas Cook, European Timetable, Peterborough, United Kingdom.
Trains. Waukesha, Wis.
Vintage Rails. Waukesha, Wis. [no longer published]

Brochures, Catalogues, Manuals, Pamphlets, Rulebooks, and Timetables

Association of American Railroads. *American Railway Signaling Principles and Practices.* New York, 1937.
Bessemer and Lake Erie Railroad Company, *Special Instructions and Operating Rules*, 1995.
Boston & Albany Railroad, *Time-Table No. 174.* 1955.
Boston and Maine Railroad, *Time Table No. 41*, 1946.
Chicago Operating Rules Association, *Operating Guide*, 1994?
CSX Transportation, *Baltimore Division, Timetable No. 2,1987.*
————.*Signal Aspect and Indication Rules.* 2001.
D.C. Buell, The Railway Educational Bureau. *Instruction Papers Units CS.3 to CS.13; Railway Signaling.* Omaha, Nebraska, 1949.
Erie Railroad Company. *Rules of the Operating Department.* 1952.
————. *Time Table No. 53.* 1956.
General Code of Operating Rules, Fourth Edition. 2000.
General Railway Signal. *Centralized Traffic Control, Type H, Class M, Coded System, Handbook 20.* Rochester, New York, 1941.
Lehigh Valley Railroad Company. *Rules for the Government of the Operating Department.* 1940.
Long Island Rail Road, *Rules of the Operating Department*, 2001.
Metro-North Railroad, *Rules of the Operating Department*, 1999.
————.*Timetable No. 1.* 2001.
New York Central System. *Rules for the Government of the Operating Department.* 1937.
New York and Long Branch Railroad. *Automatic Block and Interlocking Signals.* Printed 1906, reprinted 1975.
NORAC Operating Rules, 7th Edition. 2000.
Philadelphia & Reading Railway Company and Affiliated Lines. *Rules for the Government of the Operating Department.* 1915.
Richmond Fredericksburg and Potomac Railroad Company. *Timetable No. 31.* 1962.
Santa Fe *Signal Training* Vols. 1 & 2, 1977.
Southern Pacific Company. *Pacific System Time Table No. 17, Coast Division.* 1896.
Southern Pacific Lines. *Western Region Timetable 4.* 1990.

The Lehigh & Hudson River Railway Company. *Safety Rules*. 1916.

———. *Rules Governing the use of Automatic Block Signals*. 1951.

The New York, New Haven and Hartford Railroad. *Rules for the Government of the Operating Department*. 1925.

The Railway Signal Co. Ltd. *Control of Traffic on Railways*. London, no date.

Union Pacific, *System Timetable, No. 6*, 1982.

Western Maryland Railway Company, *Rules for the Government of the Operating Department*. 1939.

Internet Sources

Association of American Railroads www.aar.org
Burlington Northern Sante Fe Railway www.bnsf.com
Canadian National Railway Company www.cn.ca
Canadian Pacific www.cpr.ca
CSX Transportation www.csx.com
Florida East Coast Railway www.fecrwy.com
U. S. Department of Transportation, Federal Railroad Administration www.fra.dot.gov
Pan Am Railways www.guilfordrail.com [this is now Pan Am Railways, not guilford, now at www.panamrailways.com]
Genesee & Wyoming Inc. www.gwrr.com
Kansas City Southern www.kcsouthern.com
Missouri Department of Transportation www.modot.org
Montana Rail Link www.montanarail.com
Norfolk Southern www.nscorp.com
www.railamerica.com [no longer in service– Genesee & Wyoming now]
Railroad Signals of the US www.railroadsignals.us/rulebooks/rulebooks.htm
Union Pacific www.uprr.com

GLOSSARY

Absolute Permissive Block (APB): A system of automatic block signaling that uses permissive signals for following moves but absolute signals for opposing moves, which facilitates the flow of traffic without compromising safety.

Absolute signal: A fixed signal that must not be passed when displaying a "stop" aspect. A home signal is often also an absolute signal.

Approach aspect: A cautionary aspect often used to slow trains that are approaching a home signal displaying a "stop" aspect. In most modern rulebooks, this signal is indicated with a signal yellow light or a semaphore in a 45-degree diagonal position.

Aspect: The visual appearance of a fixed signal. The appearance of an aspect conveys an indication that has a specific meaning in accordance with a railway's rules.

Automatic block signal: A block signal that is part of an automatic block system (ABS—see below), actuated by a track circuit and designed to reflect track condition and block occupancy. It may be combined with an interlocking network.

Automatic block signal system: A network of defined blocks controlled by a track circuit and governed by automatic block signals and/or cab signals. This is commonly abbreviated as "ABS."

Block: A length of track between clearly defined limits, used to separate trains. Occupancy may be governed by fixed signals of either manual or automatic varieties, cab signal, staff, token, or written or verbal orders, as prescribed by the rules of the railway operating the line.

Block signal: A fixed signal for trains governing the entrance to a block.

Block system: A network of consecutive blocks used to separate trains by distance.

Centralized Traffic Control (CTC): An interlocked remote control system that allows an operator/dispatcher to direct train movements over a railway line by signal indication. Typically, it gives the operator control of switches, signals, and other operating devices. Originally, "CTC" was a trade name of the General Railway Signal Company but "CTC" is now applied to most such systems, regardless of manufacturer.

Color light signal: Signal hardware that uses colored lights to display aspects.

Color-position-light: Signal hardware that displays signal aspects through both the color and position of lights. Basic aspects are modified for speed signaling with colored marker lights, commonly abbreviated as "CPL."

Distant signal: A signal used preceding a home signal to give advance warning of the condition of that signal.

Fishtail: A style of semaphore blade consisting of an inverted chevron that resembles a fish tail. Often used for distant signals.

Fixed signal: A signal at a fixed location used to govern train movements.

Following movement: A train following another over the same section of track in the same direction. The opposite of an opposing movement.

Frog: The part of a switch or crossing that permits wheel flanges to cross rails at an angle.

Home signal: A fixed signal governing the entrance to a block, interlocking plant, or controlled point. In most situations, it is an absolute signal under control of a tower or dispatcher and thus must not be passed when displaying a "stop" indication. It is typically preceded by some form of distant signal.

Indication: The information given by a signal aspect.

Interlocking plant: A network of switches, signals, and locks mechanically or electrically interconnected, to ensure a predetermined order that prevents the arrangement of conflicting and opposing movements through the plant.

Interlocking signal: A signal controlled through mechanical or electrical means and interconnected with related switches and signals to prevent the arrangement of conflicting and opposing movements through an interlocking plant. Normally, such signals are absolute and thus cannot be passed when displaying a "stop" indication.

Junction: A place where tracks come together. Typically used to describe the merging or crossing of two or more routes.

Lower-quadrant semaphore: A semaphore that displays aspects in the lower quadrant.

Main line: A primary artery of a railroad, which may consist of one or more main tracks.

Main track: A track designated for running.

NORAC: Northeast Operation Rules Advisory Committee. A set of modern railroad operating rules that has been adopted by many railroads and commuter rail agencies operating in the Northeastern United States.

Normal speed: The maximum speed authorized on a line. This may vary by train type. Some railroads will post limits indicating the maximum speed at which each type of train may travel.

Opposing movement: The movement of a train made in the opposite direction to another train. The opposite of a following movement.

Permissive aspect: An aspect displayed by a manual block signal that permits movement at restricted speed into an occupied block.

Permissive signal: A fixed signal, usually in automatic block territory, that displays "stop and proceed" as its most restrictive aspect. Such signals are clearly distinguished from absolute signals by markings such as a number plate or letter markings.

Points: The movable part of a switch, used to direct wheel flanges from one set of tracks to another. In the British lexicon, the term "points" is used to describe the whole switch.

Position light: A signal that gives aspects using rows of lights to mimic aspects of upper-quadrant semaphores.

Restricting aspect: A signal aspect that authorizes a train to travel at restricted speed.

Restricted speed: A set of conditions as defined by railroad rules. NORAC defines movement at restricted speed under Rule 80, which states:

> Movement at Restricted Speed must apply the following three requirements as the method of operation:
> 1) Control the movement to permit stopping within one half the range of vision short of;
>   a) Other trains or railroad equipment occupying or fouling the track,
>   b) Obstructions,
>   c) Switches not properly lined for movement,
>   d) Derails set in the derailing position,
>   e) Any signal requiring a stop.
>   AND
> 2) Look out for broken or mis-aligned track.
>   AND
> 3) Do not exceed 20 mph outside interlocking limits and 15 mph within interlocking limits. This restriction applies to the entire movement, unless otherwise specified in the rule or instruction that requires Restricted Speed.

Rule book: A detailed list of rules that define the method of conduct regarding railway operations for the use of railway employees.

Semaphore: A traditional signal that displays aspects by the position of its arm, or blade. It may be operated by manual, mechanical, pneumatic, or electrical means and may be used in combination with colored lights.

Searchlight signal: A variety of color-light that uses a single lamp and a focused beam. Siding: A running track used for the meeting or passing of trains.

Signal: In this book, a signal generally refers to fixed signal hardware, as opposed to a sign made by an employee. In the strictest definition, a signal can be interpreted as sounds, lights, symbols, semaphores, or signs that are used to direct, govern, or control railway operations. Railway rules often do not distinguish between a fixed signal and a signal aspect.

Signal aspect: See Aspect

Slow speed: Typically 15 mph.

Spring switch: A switch that is operated by hand but that can accept trailing train movements in either position without risk of derailment. Springs automatically return the position of points to their normal position.

Spur: A side track that is not used for running. It may be used to store cars, locomotives, or other equipment.

Station: A designated location on a railroad used in control of operations and where business may be conducted. A station may include structures such as station buildings and other facilities but is not necessarily a traditional structure.

Switch: A track arrangement consisting of rails, points, and a frog that controls movement between tracks. Ordinary switches have two positions: normal and reverse. In railroad terminology, a switch may be "lined normal" or "lined reverse." If it has been in the reverse position and is moved back to the normal position, it has been "restored to normal."

Timetable: Printed schedules and special instructions regarding the movement of trains. Using the "timetable and train order" system of train control, an "employee timetable" (rather than the common variety issued for the convenience of passengers and shippers) authorized the movement of trains.

Train: An engine with, or without cars or multiple-unit passenger equipment. Traditionally, an engine and cars would have to display marker lamps or flags before being considered a train.

Train order: A paper order issued by an authorized member of railway operating staff, often a train dispatcher, that gives clear and specific instructions regarding the operations of trains. Typically issued on a standard form and may be used to modify, alter, or append operating instructions printed in an employee timetable.

Upper-quadrant semaphore: A semaphore that displays aspects in the upper quadrant.

Yard: A network of tracks used for assembling trains and/or storing cars and other railroad equipment. Movement on yard tracks is generally unsignaled and limited to restricted speed.

Yard limits: A section of line or tracks designated by yard limit signs where operations fall under distinctive rules designed to facilitate switching and related activities as well as mainline movements.

INDEX

Absolute Permissive Block system (APB), 80, 82–83, 85–87, 113
Adams & Westlake, 85
Advance Approach, 30, 32
AEM-7 905, 90
American Railway Association (ARA), 20–22, 28, 87, 119, 139
American Railway Signal Association, 108
American Railway Signaling Principles and Practices, 68, 74–75
Amtrak, 82, 90, 92, 93, 127
approach aspect, 16
Association of American Railroads (AAR), 22, 29, 43, 45
Atlanta & West Point, 75
Atlantic Coast Line, 75
Aurora Sub, 107
automatic block signal systems (ABS), 16, 23, 87, 93, 115
Automatic Train Stop, 92

Baird, M. A., 77
Baldwin 2-8-8-4 EM-1 7618, 70
Baltimore & Ohio, 17, 32, 39, 41, 70, 71, 80, 81, 128, 130, 131, 132
   Chicago Terminal, 131
   Cranberry Grade, 133
Bangs, Eddie, 114
banjo signal, 53
Belt Railway of Chicago, 39
Black, W. P., 67
Boston & Lowell, 55
Boston & Maine, 64, 113, 114, 116, 145
Boston & Worcester, 135
Brighton Park, 40
Budd rail diesel car, 88
Buffalo Division, 76
Buffalo Line, 125
Burlington, 98, 105, 113
Burlington Northern, 81
Burlington Northern Santa Fe (BNSF), 7, 92, 93, 100, 107, 112, 139, 142, 144
Burr Road Tower, 89

Canadian National, 14, 111, 113
Canadian Pacific, 14, 37, 50, 113, 130

Carouthers Tunnel, 132
Cassatt, Alexander, 70
Central of Georgia, 75
Central Railroad of New Jersey, 27, 44
Centralized Traffic Control (CTC), 79, 113–117
Chesapeake & Ohio, 18, 98, 99, 102, 103, 105, 146, 148
Chicago, Burlington & Quincy, 7, 112
Chicago, Milwaukee & St. Paul Railway, 126
Chicago & Alton, 131
Chicago & North Western (C&NW), 24, 54, 55, 105–107, 136–137
Chicago Metra, 106
Chicago Terminal Transfer Railroad, 39
Chicago Transit Authority, 59
Chicago Union Station, 126
Churchill, William M., 96–97, 120, 122
Cincinnati Division, 77
Class H-7A 2-8-8-2 1573, 148
Class M1 4-8-2 number 6887, 118–119
Claytor, Graham, 127
Coast Line, 134–135
Coleman, Clarence W., 72
Coleman, John Pressley, 43, 60, 61
Colonial, 90
color lights, 94–117
colored glass, 95–96
color-position-light (CPL), 128–133
Columbus Avenue Tower, 42
Conrail, 16, 17, 47, 74, 75, 79, 88, 104, 121, 127
Conroe Subdivision, 144
Corning Glass, 91, 96, 120
Cotton Belt, 115
Cox, J. C., 67
CP North Driftwood, 125
CSX, 8, 18, 28, 41, 74, 80, 81, 83, 84, 91, 103, 113, 129, 131, 132, 133
CSXT, 130

Danville Junction Maine, 111
Dash8-40B, 77
Delaware, Lackawanna & Western, 55, 79
Delaware & Hudson, 13, 70, 138

Delaware Division, 76
Denver Rio Grande & Western, 31

Eastern Railroad, Boston & Albany, 55
electric lights, 95
Elgin, Joliet & Eastern, 36
Erie Buffalo Line, 16
Erie Mining, 141
Erie Railroad, 35, 102, 105, 111, 117, 128, 146
   Style B, 76
   Style S, 17, 75–79
Erie-Lackawanna, 79

Farmer, John, 39
Federal Express, 86
Federal Railroad Administration, 51
Federal Railway Signal, 73
Federal Signal Company, 7, 39, 56, 62, 131
Fitchburg Division, 64
Fixed-Blade Distant Signal Approach, 144
Fonda, Percy, 116
Franklin Line, 58
Fresnel lens, 96, 108
Frisco, 75

Galveston, Harrisburg & San Antonio Railway, 38
Galveston Subdivision, 112, 142
General Electric, 131
Genesis diesel-electrics, 82
   P42 diesel electric, 93
   U18B, 111
General Railway Signal Company, 7, 9, 50, 62, 73, 85, 87, 98, 110, 112, 113, 114, 115, 131
   Model 2A, 28, 71, 80, 82, 83, 84
   Type D, 105, 107
   Type G, 105
   Type MD, 105
   Type ME, 105
   Type SA, 113
   Type U, 131, 133
   Type V, 133
   Type VA, 133
General Time Convention, 21
Genesee & Wyoming, 147
GG14938, 89

GP40-2, 134–135
grade crossings, 134–141
Grand Central Terminal, 88
Grants Pass Turn, 65
Great Northern, 81, 98, 105
Griswold Signal Company, 140–141
Gulf, Mobile & Ohio, 131

Hall, Thomas Seavey, 53
Hall disc signals, 12, 28, 53–57, 107
Hall Signal Company, 13, 53–57, 60, 61, 72–73, 131
    Style D, 60
    Style K, 73
    Style L, 73
Hall Switch & Signal, 73, 107–108
Hall-style A disc, 54
Harriman, E. H., 64
Harvard Subdivision, 106
Heinschell, Gerald, 38
Hobson, J. S., 60
Hoosier Sub, 83, 91
Houston Subdivision, 100
Hudson Division, 73, 108–109
Hudson River Railroad, 88

Illinois Central, 55, 98, 102
Illinois Central Gulf, 131
Indiana Railroad Commission, 80
Indianapolis State Street Yard, 80
Institution of Railway Signal Engineers, 119
interlocking aspects, 17–18
interlocking plants, 36
interlocking rules and aspects, 41–51
interlocking types, 39–41
Interstate Commerce Commission, 51, 77, 85, 92, 115

J1 Hudson 5310, 108–109
Jefferson Junction, 111
junction signals, 35–36

Kanawha Subdivision, 18
Kansas City Southern, 9
Kentucky & Indiana Bridge Company, 68
Kentucky & Louisville Belt Line, 68
Kopp Glass Company, 96

Lackawanna, 38, 78
Lancashire & Yorkshire Railway, 71
Lehigh & Hudson River, 86–87
Lehigh Valley, 55, 56, 98, 128

line crossings, 142
London, Brighton & South Coast Railway, 39
Long Island Rail Road, 14, 127
Loree, Leonor F., 70–72
Loree-Patenall, 40

M1A 4-8-2 6734, 88
Magnetic Signal Company, 139, 140
Main Line, 120, 122
Maine Central, 64, 97, 111, 145
manual block, 15
Mason City Subdivision, 11
Massachusetts Bay Transportation Authority (MBTA), 58, 114
Mazda lamps, 120
Metro-North, 45
Michigan Central, 55
Michigan Central Depot, 60
Middle Division, 68, 118–119
Milwaukee Road, 36, 37, 98, 126
Missouri-Kansas-Texas, 75
Model 2A, 32
Model MF dwarf signal, 9
Mohawk Division, 73
Monon, 8, 28, 83, 84
Montana Rail Link, 81
Morrison, C. H., 88
Mountain Division, 145
Mountain Subdivision, 41

National Transportation Safety Board, 127
New Albany Belt & Terminal Railway, 68
New Haven Railroad, 12, 19, 43, 45, 58, 87–91, 105
New Haven West Tower, 45
New Mexico Rail Runner Express, 92
New York Central, 19, 30, 32, 47, 48, 51, 73–74, 88, 98, 104, 105, 108, 108–109, 113, 115, 127, 142, 145, 146, 148
New York, Chicago & St. Louis, 102
New York Division, 76
New York, New Haven & Hartford, 55
New York, Ontario & Western, 63
New York, Westchester & Boston, 25, 42
Nickel Plate Road, 75, 102, 103, 104–105
Norfolk & Western, 75, 125, 127–128
Norfolk Southern, 79, 102, 104, 105, 121, 125, 127

Norfolk Southern Museum, 79
Northeast Corridor, 127
Northeast Operating Rules Advisory Committee (NORAC) rules, 36, 45, 105, 126
Northern Pacific, 81, 113
NSF Railway, 34–35

Ohio Division, 115
Ohio State Limited, 108–109
Oppelt, J. H., 102, 104
Oregon Railway & Navigation, 64
Oregon Short Line, 55, 64

P&L Junction, 147
Patenall, Frank P. J., 70–72, 128, 130, 131
Penn-Central, 89, 127
Pennsylvania Railroad (PRR), 15, 17, 18, 24, 39, 47, 58, 60, 68, 70, 76, 89, 97, 116, 118–121, 122, 123, 126, 127
Pennsylvania Station, 97
Pennsylvania Tunnel & Terminal Company, 97
permissive manual blocks, 16–17
Philadelphia & Reading, 28, 56
Phinney, R. M., 105, 107
Pittsburgh & Lake Erie, 111
Pneumatic Signal Company, 80
Portland & Western, 34–35
Portland Division, 64
position light signals, 118–133
Positive Train Control, 112

Q Tower, 41

RailTex's Central Oregon & Pacific, 65
Railway Gazette, The, 24, 56, 73, 108, 121
Railway Signal Association, 24, 28, 71, 73, 98, 119
Railway Signal Engineer, 64, 73, 85, 88, 125
Railway Signaling, 77, 92–93, 98, 102, 105, 130
Raton Pass, 92
Reading Company, 56–57, 116
    Budd rail diesel car, 26
    Crusader, 44
Rio Grande, 105, 113
Roberts, John, 25
Robinson, William, 53, 55
Rock Island Lines, 10–11, 100–101

158   Index

Rondout Tower, 36, 37
Rosenberg Railroad Museum, 39
Rudd, A.H., 24, 119–120, 121, 125

San Antonio & Arkansas Pass Railway Company, 38
Santa Fe, 30, 39, 75, 92–93, 98, 100, 108, 112, 143, 144
Santa Fe Magazine, 92
Saxby, John, 39
Saxby-Farmer, 38, 39
Schmid, J. D., 108–109
searchlights, 107–113
semaphores
    blades, 20–21
    electrogas, 68
    electropneumatic, 68
    lower-quadrant, 58–60, 63
    motor, 60–62
    two-arm, 22
    two-position, 52–65
    upper-quadrant, 66–93
    75th Street Tower, 39, 40
Shreveport Terminal Subdivision, 9
Signal 255, 78
Signal 308, 79
Signal Engineer and Railway Age Gazette, The, 86
Signal Engineer, The, 60, 64, 68, 72, 73, 76, 87, 96–97, 120
signaling basics
    block systems, 13–17
    color, 19, 24
    development of, 11–13
    philosophical differences in, 25–26
    standard codes, 23–24
    variety in, 27–28
Slater, W. W., 64
Southern, 105
Southern Pacific, 28, 29, 30, 39, 64–65, 108–109, 110, 111, 131, 134–135, 148
Siskiyou Line, 64, 65
    Tower 3, 38
Southwest Chief, 92, 93
speeds, 45–51
Spicer, V. K., 60, 61
Spredlite lens, 108
Standard Code (1905), 23
Standard Code (1912), 28–29
Standard Code (1949), 29–32, 43
Standard Time zones, 21
Stateline Tower, 130
"Stop and Proceed," 32

Super Chief, 92
Susquehanna Division, 76

"Take Siding" signals, 146, 148
Taylor Signal Company, 80
telephone train order signals, 77–79, 128, 146
Thomas, G. K., 93
three-position semaphores, 17
Toronto, Hamilton & Buffalo, 82
Tower 3, 38
Tower 17, 39
towers, 36–38
Traffic Control System (TCS), 115
Train Rules for Single Track, 23

Union Banner Signal, 55
Union Electric Signal Company, 53
Union Pacific, 10–11, 29, 39, 64, 106, 131, 149
Union Switch & Signal, 9, 18, 25, 29, 43, 53, 55, 58, 61, 64, 73, 79, 85, 97, 99, 108, 110, 115, 125, 131
    electropneumatic system, 44
    H-2 searchlight, 110–111
    Model 14, 98
    Style B, 61–62, 63, 64–65
    Style F electric interlocking machine, 42
    Style G, 133
    Style H-5, 112
    Style L, 98, 100
    Style N, 100–101
    Style P, 101
    Style R, 101, 102, 105
    Style R-2, 102, 103, 104–105
    Style S, 68–69, 74–75, 77, 92, 127–128
    Style T, 143
    Style T-2, 19, 92, 93, 100
    Style TP, 101
    Style TP-5, 10–11, 100–101
    Style TR, 101, 105
    TP-5, 96

Van Sweringen, Oris P. and Mantis J., 102
Varney, Jeff, 36

W. R. Sykes Interlocking Signal Company Ltd, 58
Wabash, 75, 112

Washington Union Terminal Company, 131
Water Level Route, 104, 108
Western Maryland, 75, 85–86
Western Pacific, 148
Westinghouse, 53, 55, 58
Wight, Sedgwick N., 80, 113
wigwags, 139
Wisconsin & Southern, 136–137
Woodlawn Junction, 88

About the Author

Brian Soloman has authored more than 50 books on railroads, including: *North American Railroad Family Trees, North American Railroads, Coal Trains, Railroads of California, Railroads of Pennsylvania, North American Railroad Bridges, Amtrak,* and *Railroad Signaling.* He is currently producing a popular railway photography blog called *Tracking the Light* (http://briansolomon.com/trackingthelight/) and divides his time between America and Europe to photograph and research railway operations. His photography has also appeared in the pages of many rail magazines, including *Trains Magazine, Railway Age, Railroad Explorer,* Germany's *Modelleisenbahner* and *Journal of the Irish Railway Record Society.*